Editor

Nancy Hoffman

Managing Editor

Karen J. Goldfluss, M.S. Ed.

Cover Artist

Brenda DiAntonis

Art Manager

Kevin Barnes

Art Director

CJae Froshay

Imaging

Rosa C. See

Publisher

Mary D. Smith, M.S. Ed.

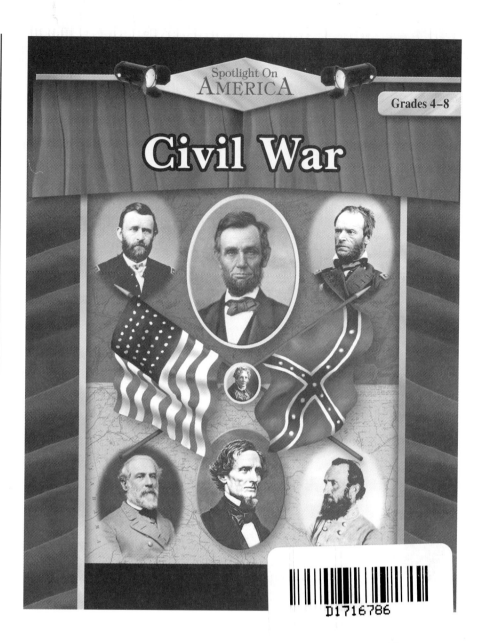

Spotlight On
AMERICA

Grades 4–8

Civil War

Author

Robert W. Smith

Teacher
Created
Resources

Teacher Created Resources, Inc.

6421 Industry Way

Westminster, CA 92683

www.teachercreated.com

ISBN-1-4206-3214-0

©*2005 Teacher Created Resources, Inc.*

Made in U.S.A.

Table of Contents

| 1650 | 1700 | 1750 | 1800 | 1850 | 1900 |

Introduction

The *Spotlight on America* series is designed to introduce some of the seminal events in American history to students in the fourth through eighth grades. Reading in the content area is enriched with a balanced variety of activities with written language, literature, poetry, social studies, and oral expression. The series is designed to make history literally come alive in your classroom and take root in the minds of your students.

The Civil War was one of the most traumatic events in American history. It was a watershed occurrence that divided the United States between its agricultural past and industrial future. More Americans—Union and Confederate—died in the Civil War than in all other U.S. wars combined. The weapons developed in that war would also be used in the First World War with even more terrible casualties for the soldiers and civilians of that conflict.

The Southern agricultural economy was destroyed and only gradually resurrected. Most of America's leaders for the next 40 years were men who had been leaders in the war. The lessons of war and peace and the bitter struggle to reconstruct the South influenced public policy and private behavior. The freed blacks were often subjected to severe mistreatment in the South under Jim Crow laws and vigilante groups like the Ku Klux Klan. The South would develop a myth of the "Lost Cause," a belief that they might or could have won if only a few events had turned out differently.

The mobilization of resources served to industrialize the North. The North barreled along, developing a powerful industrial nation powered by petroleum, steel, agricultural production, cheap immigrant labor, and the development of transcontinental railroads. The United States was soon recognized as a rapidly developing major power.

The reading selections and comprehension questions in this book introduce the Civil War. The writing and oral language activities are designed to help students sense the drama and danger which accompanied the war. Students should acquire an understanding for the urgency of events and the social, cultural, and economic milieu of the times. The research activities are intended to literally bring students into the lives and battles of people as diverse as Abraham Lincoln and Nathan Bedford Forrest, Clara Barton and Dorothea Dix, Robert E. Lee and Ulysses S. Grant. The aim of the culminating activities is to acquaint students with the life and times of people in this time period.

Enjoy using this book with your students. Look for other books in this series.

Cover Art: (top row, left to right) Ulysses S. Grant, Abraham Lincoln, William Tecumseh Sherman; (center) Harriet Beecher Stowe; (bottom row) Robert E. Lee, Jefferson Davis, Thomas "Stonewall" Jackson

Teacher Lesson Plans for Reading Comprehension

Causes of the Civil War

Objective: Students will demonstrate fluency and comprehension in reading historically based text.

Materials: copies of Causes of the Civil War (pages 7–11); copies of Causes of the Civil War Quiz (page 33); additional reading selections from books, encyclopedias, and Internet sources for enrichment

Procedure

1. Reproduce and distribute Causes of the Civil War (pages 7–11). Review pre-reading skills by briefly reviewing the text and encouraging students to underline, make notes in the margins, list questions, and highlight unfamiliar words as they read.
2. Have students read the article independently, in small groups, or together as a class.
3. As a class, discuss the following questions or others of your choosing.
   - What do you think was the most important cause of the Civil War? Why?
   - Why was the Kansas–Nebraska Act a bad idea?
   - Was John Brown a hero? Why or why not?
   - What do you think of Abraham Lincoln's attitude toward slavery?

Assessment: Have students complete Causes of the Civil War Quiz (page 33). Correct the quiz together.

Civil War Leaders from the North and the South

Objective: Students will demonstrate fluency and comprehension in reading historically based text.

Materials: copies of Civil War Leaders from the North (pages 12–14) and Civil War Leaders from the South (pages 15–17); copies of Civil War Leaders from the North Quiz (page 34) and Civil War Leaders from the South Quiz (page 35); additional reading selections from books, encyclopedias, and Internet sources for enrichment

Procedure

1. Reproduce and distribute Civil War Leaders from the North (pages 12–14). Review pre-reading skills by briefly reviewing the text and encouraging students to underline, make notes in the margins, list questions, and highlight unfamiliar words as they read.
2. Have students read the article independently, in small groups, or together as a class.
3. As a class, discuss the following questions or others of your choosing.
   - Who was the greatest Union general of the Civil War? Why?
   - Which general showed the most determination and willpower during the war?
   - How would you rank Abraham Lincoln among U.S. presidents? Why?
4. On a different day, use the above procedures for Civil War Leaders from the South (pages 15–17).
5. As a class, discuss the following questions or others of your choosing.
   - Who was the greatest Confederate general of the Civil War? Why?
   - Which general showed the most determination and willpower during the war?

Assessment: Have students complete Civil War Leaders from the North Quiz (page 34) and Civil War Leaders from the South Quiz (page 35). Correct the quizzes together.

Teacher Lesson Plans for Reading Comprehension *(cont.)*

Civil War Battles 1

Objective: Students will demonstrate fluency and comprehension in reading historically based text.

Materials: copies of Civil War Battles 1 (pages 18–20); copies of Civil War Battles 1 Quiz (page 36); additional reading selections from books, encyclopedias, and Internet sources for enrichment

Procedure

1. Reproduce and distribute Civil War Battles 1 (pages 18–20). Review pre-reading skills by briefly reviewing the text and encouraging students to underline, make notes in the margins, list questions, and highlight unfamiliar words as they read.

2. Have students read the article independently, in small groups, or together as a class.

3. As a class, discuss the following questions or others of your choosing.
   • How did the Confederate forces win against the Union forces?
   • What advantages did the Union have in the war?
   • What advantages did the South have in the war?

Assessment: Have students complete Civil War Battles 1 Quiz (page 36). Correct the quiz together.

Civil War Battles 2

Objective: Students will demonstrate fluency and comprehension in reading historically based text.

Materials: copies of Civil War Battles 2 (pages 21–23); copies of Civil War Battles 2 Quiz (page 37); additional reading selections from books, encyclopedias, and Internet sources for enrichment

Procedure

1. Reproduce and distribute Civil War Battles 2 (pages 21–23). Review pre-reading skills by briefly reviewing the text and encouraging students to underline, make notes in the margins, list questions, and highlight unfamiliar words as they read.

2. Have students read the article independently, in small groups, or together as a class.

3. As a class, discuss the following questions or others of your choosing.
   • Which was the most important battle of the war? Why?
   • Could the South have won the war? How?
   • How were the Union forces finally able to defeat the Confederate forces?

Assessment: Have students complete Civil War Battles 2 Quiz (page 37). Correct the quiz together.

Teacher Lesson Plans for Reading Comprehension *(cont.)*

A Soldier's Life

Objective: Students will demonstrate fluency and comprehension in reading historically based text.

Materials: copies of A Soldier's Life (pages 24–29); copies of A Soldier's Life Quiz (page 38); additional reading selections from books, encyclopedias, and Internet sources for enrichment

Procedure

1. Reproduce and distribute A Soldier's Life (pages 24–29). Review pre-reading skills by briefly reviewing the text and encouraging students to underline, make notes in the margins, list questions, and highlight unfamiliar words as they read.

2. Have students read the article independently, in small groups, or together as a class.

3. As a class, discuss the following questions or others of your choosing.

   • What were the three greatest dangers faced by Civil War soldiers?
   • How has the life of a soldier changed since the Civil War?
   • Why did men join the army on either side during the Civil War?
   • How have weapons and warfare changed since the Civil War?

Assessment: Have students complete A Soldier's Life Quiz (page 38). Correct the quiz together.

Reconstruction

Objective: Students will demonstrate fluency and comprehension in reading historically based text.

Materials: copies of Reconstruction (pages 30–32); copies of Reconstruction Quiz (page 39); additional reading selections from books, encyclopedias, and Internet sources for enrichment

Procedure

1. Reproduce and distribute Reconstruction (pages 30–32). Review pre-reading skills by briefly reviewing the text and encouraging students to underline, make notes in the margins, list questions, and highlight unfamiliar words as they read.

2. Have students read the article independently, in small groups, or together as a class.

3. As a class, discuss the following questions or others of your choosing.

   • How were freed blacks cheated out of their rights during and after Reconstruction?
   • If Lincoln had lived, would he have been more successful in rebuilding the South and helping the former slaves? Why or why not?
   • Why did many Southerners fear the education of blacks?

Assessment: Have students complete Reconstruction Quiz (page 39). Correct the quiz together.

 Reading Passages

Causes of the Civil War

Slavery

The root cause of the American Civil War was slavery. African laborers had been imported into the colony of Jamestown within a few years of its founding in 1607. Unlike indentured servants from England and other European countries, Africans soon became permanent slave laborers with no protected human rights. Slavery spread through all of the English colonies, but it became essential to the agricultural economy of the Southern colonies.

Some settlers in the Northern colonies owned black slaves who worked on their small farms. Often the slaves became household servants or helped craftsmen, mill owners, and other tradesmen who often taught these trades to their slaves. Some of these slaves eventually earned or were granted their freedom. Slaves never made up a large part of the population in the Northern states.

Southern Plantation Economy

In the Southern colonies, slavery was a very important part of the economy. New Englander Eli Whitney's invention of the hand-cranked cotton gin in 1793 made slavery of blacks especially profitable. The gin combed the fiber and separated the seeds from cotton fiber much faster than could be done by hand. This invention encouraged plantation owners to raise huge crops of cotton which were grown and harvested with slave labor.

Cotton became the basis of the Southern economy and was a huge cash crop exported to the Northern states and Europe.

In many Southern states, slaves were as numerous as whites. There were five million Southern whites and four million black slaves when the Civil War began in 1861.

The "Peculiar Institution"

The Southern states became very sensitive about their "peculiar institution" (slavery). Some Southerners, led by John C. Calhoun who was vice president under Andrew Jackson, believed that states' rights were more important than federal authority and declared that a state could refuse to obey any federal law with which it did not agree. President Jackson and those who believed in the supremacy of the Constitution and federal laws were opposed to the idea.

Reading Passages

Causes of the Civil War *(cont.)*

The Abolitionists

In the mid-1830s, a number of powerful voices were being raised in the North calling for a complete end to slavery and especially for *the abolition*, or elimination, of slavery in any newly created states. Abolitionists cited a "higher law" greater than the Constitution.

William Lloyd Garrison was a leading abolitionist who started publishing a newspaper in 1931 named *The Liberator,* which called for the immediate abolition of slavery. He was considered an extremist, but he did influence many citizens and helped organize opposition to slavery. A pro-slavery mob wrecked his printing press and set his house on fire. Mobs attacked anti-slavery supporters and suspected enemies in many Southern and Western communities.

Ralph Waldo Emerson, Wendell Phillips, Louisa May Alcott, and many other New England writers and religious leaders supported the abolitionist cause. Frederick Douglass, an escaped slave who later bought his own freedom, became a powerful voice calling for an end to slavery. Sojourner Truth, a freed black woman, gave speeches throughout the North and West opposing slavery. Other radical newspaper publishers, religious, and college leaders condemned slavery as evil. Gradually these voices convinced many Northerners that slavery must be ended and made Southerners believe that they could no longer work with the North.

Uncle Tom's Cabin

Harriet Beecher Stowe, an author from an important family of preachers, wrote a book about slavery that described the harsh treatment of slaves and portrayed white owners as brutal, evil people who cruelly abused their slaves. *Uncle Tom's Cabin* was first published in installments in 1851 in an abolitionist paper and the next year in book form. Stowe wrote the book as an argument against the Fugitive Slave Laws (see page 9).

Southerners were furious at *Uncle Tom's Cabin,* possibly because it brought home many of the evils of the slave system. The book was an immediate bestseller in the North as well as in England and Europe. Publication of the book did a great deal to unify Northern sentiment against slavery and to divide the states even more.

The importance of the book was noted by President Lincoln who, when introduced to Harriet Beecher Stowe said, "So this is the little lady who wrote the book that made this great war!"

Reading Passages

Causes of the Civil War *(cont.)*

Free States vs. Slave States

At first only radical abolitionists wanted to get rid of slavery in the Southern states where it existed, but many Northerners were opposed to the expansion of slavery into new states. The Missouri Compromise of 1820, proposed by Kentucky Congressman Henry Clay, admitted Missouri as a slave state and Maine as a free state, thereby setting a practice of admitting an equal number of free and slave states and keeping a balance of power between the Northern and Southern states. The Compromise of 1850, also designed by Clay, allowed California to enter the Union as a free state and the new states of Utah and New Mexico to decide for themselves whether they would be free or slave.

Kansas–Nebraska Act

In 1854 Senator Stephen A. Douglas from Illinois helped pass the Kansas–Nebraska Act. This law provided that citizens in the new states could decide for themselves whether they would be free or slave states. Many Northern citizens were furious at this act, which brought an end to compromise and led to increased violence especially in Kansas.

Bleeding Kansas

Kansas became a battleground before the Civil War actually began as Southerners from Missouri and other states clashed with Northerners from many states.

Radicals from both sides went to Kansas to help fight and vote. Both groups got into violent conflicts, and people on both sides of the issue were whipped, abused, lynched, and shot. Homes and farms were burned, many businesses were destroyed, and elections were not conducted fairly.

Fugitive Slave Laws

Henry Clay included language in the Compromise of 1850 which strengthened the Fugitive Slave Laws, requiring Northern citizens and Northern law officers to return escaped slaves to their owners. It included a huge $1,000 fine and six months jail time for people who refused to cooperate. Southern slave hunters often traveled through border states and free states, capturing not only escaped slaves, but free blacks as well, and then taking them South. The Fugitive Slave Laws caused widespread anger, increased participation in the Underground Railroad, and helped widen the divide between the North and South.

Reading Passages

Causes of the Civil War *(cont.)*

Underground Railroad

The *Underground Railroad* was not a railroad at all. It was an escape route for fugitive slaves, and the "stations" were hiding places. Slaves who decided to run from their owners were aided by several people in Southern communities, border state residents, and Northern opponents of slavery. Runaway slaves were hidden under loads in wagons and in barn lofts, cellars, secret rooms, abandoned buildings, caves, sheds, and closets.

These slaves were usually hidden during the day and moved at night from one station to another as they traveled from slave and border states through Northern states to Canada.

One of the most famous "conductors," or leaders, of the Underground Railroad was Harriet Tubman. She was an escaped slave who eventually led more than 400 fugitive slaves to freedom.

Many *Quakers*, a religious group opposed to slavery and violence, were also deeply involved in this effort. One Quaker named Levi Coffin helped organize the Underground Railroad and personally assisted in the escape of more than 1,000 fugitive slaves.

Dred Scott Decision

Dred Scott was a slave who lived with his master, an army officer, in Illinois and Wisconsin which were free states and in Missouri which was a slave state. When his master died in Missouri, Scott sued for his freedom on the basis that he had traveled and lived in free states and thus should be free. The case attracted national attention when it hit the courts because it pitted the North directly against the South.

The case ended up in the U.S. Supreme Court. Chief Justice Roger Taney ruled against Scott and stated that no black— free or slave—could sue in federal court because blacks were not and could not be citizens according to the Constitution, and it did not matter where they lived. The ruling said that a slave could not be free just because he or she was in a free state.

Reading Passages

Causes of the Civil War *(cont.)*

John Brown

John Brown, a radical abolitionist, had gone to Kansas and killed at least five pro-slavery men and committed other acts of violence. Brown was a supporter of slave rebellions and believed that slavery would only be removed by violent action. In 1859 he and a small group of followers invaded Harpers Ferry, a federal storehouse for weapons in what is now West Virginia, and called for a general slave rebellion.

Most of Brown's followers were quickly killed by armed citizens and soldiers who surrounded the arsenal. Brown and a few followers were captured by federal troops commanded by Robert E. Lee. Brown was quickly tried, convicted of murder and treason, and hanged. His trial energized the Northern opponents of slavery and angered Southern supporters of slavery, creating deeper divisions in an already divided nation.

Lincoln's Election: A House Divided

In a famous speech, Abraham Lincoln had said that "a house divided against itself cannot stand." He said the "house"—the United States—could not survive being half slave and half free. The country would eventually have to choose. The choice came in 1860.

Northern Democrats nominated Illinois Senator Stephen A. Douglas for president.

Southern Democrats, who were unwilling to accept any Northerner, nominated John C. Breckinridge of Kentucky. The Constitutional Union party ran John Bell of Tennessee. The new Republican Party picked Lincoln, who had become quite famous in the North and was disliked in the South for the series of debates he participated in when he ran for the U.S. Senate in 1858 and lost to Douglas. Lincoln ran on a policy of preserving the Union, allowing slavery to exist where it already existed and opposing slavery in newly created states. Lincoln was so disliked in the South that he was not even on the ballot in 10 Southern states. Nonetheless, in a four-way race he won 40 percent of the vote and gained a majority of the electoral votes.

Secession

Soon after Lincoln's election victory, Southerners (fearful of his opposition to slavery) decided that secession (separating) from the Union was the only solution. Lincoln was elected in November 1860 and scheduled to be inaugurated on March 4, 1861. South Carolina seceded on December 20 and by March 4, 1861, six other states had seceded and formed the Confederacy. When Fort Sumter was attacked on April 12, four other states including Virginia joined to make a Confederacy of 11 states.

Civil War Leaders from the North

Abraham Lincoln

Regarded by many Americans as one of the greatest U.S. presidents, Lincoln had the difficult job of keeping the country united during the Civil War. Born into extreme poverty, he educated himself and tried his hand at several businesses in which he failed. He became a lawyer and a successful legislator before he became the presidential nominee of the new Republican Party. Lincoln saw most of the Southern states secede between the time of his election in November 1860 and his inauguration as president in March 1861. A month later, the Civil War began with the firing on Fort Sumter by Confederate forces.

Lincoln led the country through four long years of war with terrible casualties on both sides. Although personally opposed to slavery as a moral evil, he had been willing to allow slavery where it already existed if that policy would keep the Union together. After the war began, Lincoln gradually realized that freeing the slaves was part of the path to victory, and he issued the Emancipation Proclamation in January 1863. This act encouraged many slaves in Southern states to flee from their owners.

The tide of war often seemed to favor the Confederate forces, and Lincoln's opponent in 1864 ran on a peace platform favoring separation into two countries.

The capture of Atlanta and other Union successes in the fall of 1864 led to Lincoln's reelection. Just five days after the surrender at Appomattox, he was assassinated while attending a play at Ford's Theater.

Ulysses S. Grant

Ulysses S. Grant was commander of the Union Army. He had an unimpressive record at West Point and later served in several army posts. He was charged at one western post for drinking too much. Grant eventually left the army in 1854 and spent the next six years failing as a farmer, a real estate agent, and a clerk. He was reduced to working in the family tannery, a job he hated, when the war broke out. He was soon appointed a colonel and later brigadier general with victories at Fort Henry and Fort Donelson in Tennessee.

His troops won a costly victory at Shiloh and after a month of determined siege, captured Vicksburg. Lincoln made him general in chief of all the Union Armies. He fought Confederate General Robert E. Lee in a series of bloody conflicts at Spotsylvania, Cold Harbor, the Wilderness Campaign, and the siege of Petersburg. Union General William Tecumseh Sherman's victory at Atlanta and the collapse of Lee's forces led to final victory. After the war, Grant served as commander of the Army. He was elected president of the United States in 1868.

Reading Passages

Civil War Leaders from the North *(cont.)*

William Tecumseh Sherman

William Tecumseh Sherman was a Union general. An Ohio-born graduate of West Point, he fought in the Mexican War, worked as a banker and military school superintendent, and rejoined the army when war began.

Sherman led troops at the disastrous battle of Bull Run. At one point early in the war, he lost his command and even considered suicide. Sherman had difficulty with most of his superiors, except his friend Ulysses S. Grant. He disliked politicians, distrusted newspapermen, and believed that "war is all hell."

In March 1862, Sherman received command of the 5th Division, Army of the Tennessee, and fought bravely at Shiloh, Tennessee. He served with Grant in the battles leading up to the capture of Vicksburg, Mississippi. He directed the attack that led to the city's surrender. In 1864, Sherman succeeded Grant as commander of most of the western forces. He marched east to capture Atlanta, Georgia. After a summer of long sieges and bitter fighting, Sherman's forces captured Atlanta. This was a critical battle because it clearly indicated the decline of the Confederacy and led to the reelection of Abraham Lincoln. Sherman then began his famous march from Atlanta to the sea, cutting off Confederate supply lines of food and war materials. He captured Savannah, Georgia, in December.

George B. McClellan

Union General George McClellan was a West Point graduate, a hero of the Mexican War, a railroad executive, and an acquaintance of Abraham Lincoln before the war. When the war began, he became a major general and helped keep Kentucky and West Virginia in the Union. In late 1861, Lincoln appointed him general in chief of the army. McClellan was thorough in his preparations and outstanding in organizing the new troops into a well-drilled, disciplined, proud army.

General McClellan was extremely cautious in fighting the enemy and always claimed he needed more troops or more supplies. Lincoln was so frustrated by McClellan's caution that he even asked if he could borrow his army since McClellan was not using it. McClellan was eventually removed from command and replaced by other generals who were not much more successful than he was until Grant was appointed.

 Reading Passages

Civil War Leaders from the North *(cont.)*

Clara Barton

Clara Barton, who became known as the "Angel of the Battlefield," was a former school teacher and a Patent Office clerk when the war began. She became a volunteer nurse for wounded soldiers and then expanded her efforts to bring supplies and other volunteers right onto the battlefields. Eventually, Barton took charge of some Union hospitals and toward the end of the war led the search for Union men who were missing in action. She later created the American branch of the Red Cross to help in times of war and natural disasters.

John Brown

John Brown was a fierce abolitionist who devoted much of his adult life to the antislavery cause. He and five of his sons moved to Kansas in order to fight the pro-slavery forces, which resulted in the deaths of five pro-slavery men. Brown considered himself an instrument of God, chosen to lead slaves in a rebellion against slavery. In October 1859, he and 21 followers attacked a government armory at Harpers Ferry, expecting slaves to rise up and join him. The expected slave uprising did not happen. Most of his men were killed, and he was captured, convicted, and hanged for treason. His actions and statements helped convince many Northerners that he was right and also convinced many Southerners that future compromise was impossible. Brown became the subject of a famous song which began, "John Brown's body lies a-mould'ring in the grave."

Frederick Douglass

An escaped slave who later bought his own freedom, Frederick Douglass was the most famous black man of his time. He became a powerful speaker against the evils of slavery, traveled to England as a lecturer, and was a friend to most of the antislavery people of his day, including John Brown. He helped convince President Lincoln to allow blacks to serve as soldiers, and he strongly supported the efforts of former slaves to achieve full civil rights.

Philip Henry Sheridan

General Philip Henry Sheridan was an extremely competent cavalry officer who eventually took charge of the Army of the Potomac under Grant's command. He fought with skill and discipline at Chickamauga, Georgia, and Chattanooga, Tennessee. Assuming command of the Army of the Shendandoah in 1864, he destroyed rebel property and supplies and defeated General Jubal Anderson Early's Confederate forces in several battles. His cavalry troops surrounded part of Lee's army at Appomattox, forcing the Confederates to surrender.

Reading
Passages

Civil War Leaders from the South

Jefferson Davis

President of the Confederate States of America (CSA), Jefferson Davis was a West Point graduate, Mississippi plantation owner, U.S. congressman, soldier in the Black Hawk Indian War and the Mexican War, U.S. senator, and secretary of war. Davis was a dedicated supporter of the Southern position on slavery and its expansion into new states. He opposed secession and favored compromise until the election of Lincoln and southern secession led to his resignation from the Senate.

Davis was elected president of the Confederacy as a compromise candidate and spent much of the war frustrated by the independent attitude of the Southern states. These states were unwilling to surrender their control over supplies and volunteer armies. They would not agree to a draft, the creation of a slave army, or common military actions. Davis often disagreed with individual Southern commanders, who were unimpressed by his military advice. He was a close friend of West Point classmate Robert E. Lee. At war's end, Davis was captured by Union troops. He was imprisoned and later charged with treason but never tried. He never accepted a federal pardon.

Robert E. Lee

The son of Revolutionary War hero "Lighthorse" Harry Lee, Robert E. Lee was the commander in chief of the Confederate Army and helped Jefferson Davis direct Southern war planning. Lee was an honored graduate of West Point and a hero of the Mexican War. He was so admired by military men that Lincoln offered him command of the Northern armies. Despite his discomfort with states' rights and slavery, Lee felt he had to defend his home state of Virginia and therefore resigned from the U.S. Army.

Lee and Stonewall Jackson made a brilliant team. They forced the withdrawal of Union forces from Richmond and won a series of victories at Second Bull Run, Fredericksburg, and Chancellorsville, where Jackson was killed. Lee decided to invade the North and pushed into Pennsylvania, where he was defeated after heavy losses at Gettysburg. Lee retreated to Virginia and fought on against Grant in the Wilderness Campaign. The overwhelming advantages of the North in men, weapons, and supplies led to the gradual destruction of Lee's army, and he was forced to surrender to Grant at Appomattox Court House on April 9, 1865, ending the war. After the war he urged Southerners to accept the results and rebuild their homes and businesses. Lee served as the president of a small college for several years.

 Reading Passages

Civil War Leaders from the South *(cont.)*

Thomas "Stonewall" Jackson

Thomas Jackson was a West Point graduate with a record of heroism and skill earned during the Mexican War. An instructor at the Virginia Military Institute when the Civil War began, Jackson was soon appointed brigadier general.

After standing like a stone wall against Union attacks in the first battle of Bull Run, he earned the nickname "Stonewall" Jackson, and he also became commander of the Army of the Shenandoah Valley.

His ability to march his men for long distances and then fight the enemy earned him great respect. Jackson and Lee made a superb team. Jackson's units often marched around the Union army to attack the rear or disrupted Northern forces so that his Confederate troops could destroy them one regiment at a time. Jackson was accidentally shot by one of his own men in May 1863 at Chancellorsville, Virginia. His arm was amputated, and he died eight days later. At the loss of this able commander, General Lee commented that Jackson was simply irreplaceable.

James Longstreet

General James Longstreet was known as "Old War Horse." A West Point graduate, Longstreet resigned from the U.S. Army in 1861 to fight for the Confederate cause. He led troops at the First Battle of Bull Run, the Peninsular Campaign, and Fredericksburg. As Lee's "Old War Horse," he commanded the right wing of the army at Gettysburg. After the defeat of Lee's forces, Longstreet was often blamed by Southerners because he felt that a defensive strategy would be more effective and had been cautious in attacking the Union positions. Longstreet fought at Lee's side until the surrender at Appomattox.

 Reading Passages

Civil War Leaders from the South *(cont.)*

John Hunt Morgan

General John Hunt Morgan was a Confederate cavalry leader famous for his daring, speed, and determination. He organized his own Kentucky Cavalry and led raids against Union forces in Kentucky, Tennessee, Mississippi, Indiana, and Ohio. His men captured thousands of prisoners, destroyed property, and collected tons of food, ammunition, and other supplies. They severely disrupted Union supply trains and communications. Large units of Union troops were occupied in trying to capture Morgan. He escaped from a Union prison after being captured and continued his raids until he was killed in an attack in Tennessee.

John Singleton Mosby

John Singleton Mosby joined the Confederate army as a private and was later made an officer assigned to lead scouting missions for General J.E.B. Stuart. In 1863 he organized his own cavalry unit called Mosby's Rangers, a daring unit of Confederate cavalry troops who followed his personal leadership. Known as "The Gray Ghost," he harassed Union troops in the area around Washington, DC; Maryland; and Virginia. He disrupted Union troop movements, captured supplies, and occupied the attentions of many Union forces trying to capture him.

Nathan Bedford Forrest

A poor man who became a plantation owner through hard work, Nathan Bedford Forrest raised his own cavalry force at the beginning of the war and fought in many battles including Ft. Donelson, Shiloh, and Chickamauga. He was famous for his ability to move his men rapidly, arriving as he said, "fustest with the mostest." Once trapped on two flanks by Union forces, General Forrest divided his men and ordered them to charge both ways. They did and escaped the trap.

Reading Passages

Civil War Battles 1

Fort Sumter

Fort Sumter was a federal fort in the harbor at Charleston, South Carolina, a state which had seceded from the Union and joined the Confederacy. President Lincoln informed Governor Francis Wilkinson Pickens of South Carolina of his intention to resupply the fort. Jefferson Davis, president of the Confederacy, decided that the fort must not be resupplied and ordered its capture.

Confederate General Pierre Gustave Toutant Beauregard ordered the bombardment of Fort Sumter early in the morning on April 12, 1861. The cannons fired for two days while Union forces held out. Major Robert Anderson, the Union commander of the fort, was short of ammunition, food, and men. Unable to prevent the fort's capture, he was forced to surrender the fort on April 14. The news of Fort Sumter's capture caused Lincoln to call for 75,000 volunteers to retake federal property. Virginia, Arkansas, North Carolina, and Tennessee promptly seceded and joined the Confederacy. The country was at war.

The First Battle of Bull Run (Manassas)

Citizens in both the Union and Confederacy thought the war would be short and swift with few casualties. Young men on both sides were eager to volunteer to fight. They were afraid they would miss the entire war if they did not enlist right away. The Confederates wanted another quick victory to boost Southern moral and convince the North to make peace. The Union commander, General Irvin McDowell, wanted to get his men into battle before their 90-day enlistment period was up.

On the morning of July 21, 1861, McDowell attacked the Southern fortifications at Manassas Junction in Virginia. Union troops were poorly trained and lightly equipped. They expected an easy victory. Ladies and gentlemen in buggies, children, Congressmen, reporters, and other civilians (often carrying picnic lunches) followed the army to watch the battle. The battle was a confusion of small fights and inexperienced combat on both sides. The Northern forces were routed and forced to retreat right through the ranks of the civilian spectators. It was a serious defeat for the North and an indication that this war would not be easy.

Reading Passages

Civil War Battles 1 *(cont.)*

Fort Donelson

Fort Donelson was an important Confederate fort guarding the Cumberland River near the Kentucky–Tennessee border. Union forces, led by the then unknown Brigadier General Ulysses S. Grant, attacked the fort in February 1862. They managed to surround the fort with gunboats on the river side and troops around the landward side. The Confederates attempted to break out in the middle of a snowstorm, which hid their attack. Although Union forces were

pushed back almost a mile, the exhausted Rebels were forced to retreat and surrendered unconditionally to Grant on February 16, 1862. Grant became a Northern hero with the nickname "Unconditional Surrender" (U.S.) Grant. This was the first major Union victory of the war and opened the deep South to attack by Union forces.

Naval Battles at Hampton Roads

The Confederates built an ironclad ship to help smash the blockade of their ports by the Union. The *Virginia* (often called the *Merrimack*) looked like a floating, iron barn. On March 8, 1862, the *Virginia* sailed out of Norfolk to attack Union ships blockading the port. Despite its very slow speed, it managed to ram and sink one ship and destroy two other ships with cannon fire. Union cannon balls bounced off the ship without effect. The next day, a Union ironclad named the *Monitor* arrived, and the two ships dueled for hours without a clear winner. Naval warfare changed with this battle, however, and the days of the wooden ship were numbered.

Shiloh (Pittsburg Landing)

The Confederates launched an unexpected attack on General Grant's forces near Pittsburg Landing and Shiloh Church in Tennessee. The Confederates managed to force the Union troops back after 12 hours of bloody warfare on April 6, 1862. That night Grant refused to retreat. General Sherman rallied Union troops, and the next day they fought back. The Confederates were forced to retreat, and Shiloh was another costly Union victory. Shiloh was one of the bloodiest battles of the war. Union losses were over 13,000 while Confederate losses were over 10,000 soldiers.

Reading Passages

Civil War Battles 1 *(cont.)*

The Second Battle of Bull Run (Manassas)

After months of sparring between Union forces led by General George McClellan and the Army of Northern Virginia led by General Robert E. Lee, the Union Army had been outmaneuvered, defeated, and pushed back out of much of Virginia. Lincoln tried a new commander, General John Pope. Pope was tricked into an attack on Stonewall Jackson's troops on August 29, 1862. Jackson's troops appeared to be beaten, but Lee sent reinforcements to attack the Union's left flank. Union troops broke rank and ran until a determined defense was organized just 20 miles from Washington. It was another bitter defeat for the Union.

Antietam (Sharpsburg)

In September 1892, Lee marched his troops into Maryland hoping to achieve a Confederate victory and gain British recognition of the Confederate States as a nation. On September 17, 1862, Lee's 18,000 troops, backed up against Antietam Creek near the town of Sharpsburg, were attacked by some of McClellan's 95,000 Union troops. The attack was poorly designed and disorganized, but the fighting was bloody. Union forces were unable to defeat or destroy the Army of Northern Virginia, but they did halt its advance into the North. This was the single bloodiest day of the war with over 23,000 casualties.

Fredericksburg

The new commander of the Union forces, General Ambrose Burnside, hoped to capture Richmond and end the war. Delayed for a week until pontoon bridges arrived, Burnside ordered his men to attack Lee's forces which were dug in on the high ground overlooking Fredericksburg, Virginia. The attack on the well-defended Confederates resulted in almost 13,000 Union casualties. The entrenched rebels had about 5,300 casualties. Burnside was forced to order his men to retreat, and the Northern forces suffered another defeat.

Reading Passages

Civil War Battles 2

Chancellorsville

The new Union commander, "Fighting Joe" Hooker, was popular with his troops and eager to meet the Confederates in battle. In May 1863, he attacked the 60,000-man Confederate army at Chancellorsville, Virginia, with his 130,000 troops. Hooker was repeatedly outmaneuvered by Generals Robert E. Lee and Stonewall Jackson, who positioned their men so that they always had equal or superior numbers at the point of attack. After three days of fighting, Hooker's troops were beaten, and he was forced to retreat. Despite his brilliant military maneuvers, Lee lost 13,000 men and his best commander. Jackson was wounded in battle and died a week later.

Vicksburg

Vicksburg was the last Southern stronghold on the Mississippi River. General Ulysses S. Grant was determined to take the city and cut the Confederacy in half. Despite the destruction of much of his supply line by Confederate forces, Grant marched his men over 180 miles in 17 days, fought five major battles, and surrounded the city. His artillery pounded the city until July 4, 1863, when Vicksburg finally surrendered. By this time, its weary citizens and defending army were both starving. Control of this city gave the Union forces control of the Mississippi River.

Gettysburg

Hoping to bring the war to an end, General Lee decided to invade the North again and take advantage of the war weariness of Union citizens. Confederate and Union forces clashed by accident at Gettysburg, a small town in Pennsylvania.

During three days of brutal warfare, Lee tried to destroy the Union armies and convince the North to accept the division of the country. Fighting with fewer men, less supplies, and unable to secure a military advantage on the ground, Lee's army was halted and defeated by Union forces.

The final effort—an attack by Confederate General George Pickett's troops—failed. Lee was forced to retreat back to Virginia, having suffered over 28,000 casualties. Union dead and wounded numbered over 23,000.

 Reading Passages

Civil War Battles 2 *(cont.)*

Chickamauga and Chattanooga

In September 1863, Union forces under General William Rosecrans clashed with Confederate General Braxton Bragg's army at Chickamauga Creek in northwest Georgia. During the battle, Rosecrans ordered some of his troops to shift positions to fill what he believed was a break in the Union lines. In the shift, his army left a huge gap in the lines, and Confederate forces were able to attack and force the retreat of the entire Union army. At Chattanooga, Tennessee, the Union forces were surrounded by Confederate forces.

With Grant now in command of all Union troops and tough Union commanders in charge of divisions at Chattanooga, Union troops overcame strong Confederate resistance. They attacked a superior Confederate stronghold at Missionary Ridge, turned the tide, and gave the Union a brilliant victory.

The Wilderness, Spotsylvania, and Cold Harbor

General Grant was now in control of all the Union forces. His army fought with Lee's army in a series of bloody battles in the Wilderness (a thick patch of woods near Chancellorsville), at Spotsylvania; and Cold Harbor—all located in Virginia. The battles were extremely bitter, very costly in terms of casualties, and provided no victories. Grant's army suffered almost

50,000 casualties and Lee's about 32,000. Both commanders lost nearly half of their armies. The South was running out of men, but the North seemed to have an endless supply.

The Battle of Atlanta

On July 22, 1864, Union General William Sherman laid siege to the city of Atlanta, Georgia, with the intent of breaking the back of the Confederacy. In six weeks of bitter fighting, the Union forces gradually surrounded the city of Atlanta and wore down the defending Confederate army. The Confederate army was barely able to escape before Sherman's troops completely surrounded the city in late August.

On September 2, 1864, Sherman entered Atlanta. The defeat of Atlanta convinced the war-weary North that the end of the war was in sight and also led to the reelection of Lincoln in November.

Civil War Battles 2 *(cont.)*

The March to the Sea

After taking Atlanta, General Sherman took 62,000 men and marched across Georgia to the sea. He was determined to destroy the South's ability to wage war and feed her armies. He created a path of destruction, sometimes as wide as 60 miles, and destroyed at least 100 million dollars in property. The army captured food, freed slaves, destroyed railroad lines, and burned many farms. Sherman's army captured Savannah, Georgia, on December 21, 1864, which he offered to President Lincoln as a Christmas gift.

Petersburg

The last great campaign of the war was the siege of Petersburg, a communications center about 20 miles south of Richmond, Virginia. After his army failed to capture the city, Grant's troops surrounded the city and laid siege to it for 10 months. They tried to blast their way through Confederate fortifications in late July 1864 and almost succeeded before Confederate troops filled the gap and held off the Union advance. The continued pressure of Grant's troops forced Lee to abandon Petersburg and leave Richmond, the capital of the Confederacy, open to capture by Grant's forces.

Surrender at Appomattox

General Lee's attempt to link up with other Southern armies was halted by Union cavalry at Appomattox Station in Virginia. Lee determined that his men no longer had any serious hope of victory. They were out of food, short of ammunition, and their numbers terribly reduced by the long years of fighting.

Grant accepted Lee's surrender at the home of Wilmer McLean in the town of Appomattox Court House on April 9, 1865. Grant was generous in his surrender terms. He allowed the officers and men to return to their homes and offered food to the half-starved rebel army. The formal surrender of the troops occurred three days later. The war was over, although some minor clashes still occurred in the next few weeks.

 Reading Passages

A Soldier's Life

Joining the Army

The median age of the soldiers in the Civil War was 24 years old. Half of the soldiers were younger and half older. Soldiers in the Union army were supposed to be 18 years old, but many young men lied about their age and entered the army at 16 or 17. A few were even younger. Many men over the age of 45 also enlisted. As the war dragged on, the South began to have many soldiers who were older.

In the first few weeks of the war, Union troops were volunteers who joined state regiments. Southern volunteers also flocked to their local and state militias. After the first burst of patriotism, volunteers were fewer, and the Union offered cash bonuses to men who signed up.

As the war dragged on and casualties mounted, both sides resorted to *conscription*, drafting men to fight. In both the South and North, however, men with some occupations were exempted from the draft. In addition, Southerners who owned 20 slaves or more were exempt from the draft, although some volunteered anyway.

The wealthy were able to avoid the draft, too. In the North, a man could avoid military service by paying money to the government, and in both the North and South, a man who was drafted could hire a substitute to go in his place.

Drummer Boys

Musicians did not have to meet the minimum age requirement because they were technically noncombatants. These drummer boys and buglers were often only 12 or 13 years old. The drum beats and bugle calls were the methods used to tell soldiers when to attack during a battle. The drummers also beat time during marches and drills.

Drummer boys performed other nonmusical services. They served as water boys, barbers, cooks, and stretcher bearers. They often assisted surgeons during amputations and carried piles of legs and arms away from the surgeons' operating tables. Sometimes they helped close wounds and put on bandages. Many drummer boys were wounded or killed during the war since bullets and cannon fire did not distinguish between ages or rank.

 Reading Passages

A Soldier's Life *(cont.)*

Foreign Soldiers

Both armies had foreign volunteers. Some were officers and even generals. About nine percent of the Confederate troops were foreigners. About 25 percent of the Northern troops were foreigners, usually immigrants from European countries. There were dozens of all-German regiments in the North, and the Irish made up the majority of at least 20 regiments. Some units were a blend of many nationalities. One New York regiment included Hungarian, Spanish, French, English, and German recruits. Some foreigners joined to fight for the causes they believed in. Others joined for adventure, steady wages, or because they had no better opportunity.

Native and African-American Soldiers

Native Americans fought in large numbers on both sides of the war. The Cherokee nation was openly allied with the South, which they thought would give them better treatment after the war.

At first the Union government refused to enlist black soldiers. However, the number of casualties in 1862, the demands of abolitionists and famous black leader Frederick Douglass, and the passage of the Emancipation Proclamation led to the formation of regiments of black soldiers who fought in many battles. By the end of the war, at least 180,000 black soldiers served in the Union cause. Tens of thousands of freed blacks also helped build defenses and worked in Union army camps.

Camp Life

Although many Northern troops came from larger cities like New York, Boston, or Philadelphia, most soldiers were farm boys because the United States was still a nation of farmers. Hard work at home had prepared many of the men for the difficult life of a soldier, but some things were different. The crowded life of an army camp was new to most of the men, and they were not used to the terrible food, drills, marching, and long periods of boredom.

New recruits usually lived in army tents when they were available, but more permanent log cabins were often built for winter quarters by groups of four soldiers. These cabins were extremely crude huts, but they did lessen the cold bite of winter.

Reading
Passages

A Soldier's Life *(cont.)*

Passing Time

In the military there was less training in the winter, especially during bad weather, so the men played chess, wrote letters, wrestled, sang songs, and tried to improve the quality of their food by cooking. Men also played cards and gambled on just about anything. The soldiers bet on wrestling matches, head lice races (head lice were everywhere), baseball games, and just about anything else.

Food

The food on both sides ranged from tasteless to disgusting. Southern soldiers were often short of rations, and supplies were always irregular. This lack of basic provisions was a major reason for the Confederates' surrender at Appomattox. Southern agriculture produced food, but it did not get equally distributed to either the soldiers or people in the cities.

Except during some long marches and battles, Northern troops were well supplied, but the food was usually spoiled or of poor quality. Beef and pork were often preserved in so much salt that it had to be soaked in water for hours so that it could even be eaten.

The soldiers did their own cooking and often cooked the meat in gobs of grease, which caused numerous stomach problems. Northern troops were supplied with dehydrated vegetables, which were supposed to be dried beans, turnips, onions, carrots, and beets, but which also contained leaves, roots, and stalks. Even soaked in hot water, they were unappetizing.

"Teeth Dullers"

The Union troops made a flour and water biscuit called *hardtack*, which was so tough it was called "teeth dullers" and "sheet-iron crackers." The flour often contained weevils and other insects. Soldiers soaked this biscuit in coffee and skimmed off the insects which floated out of the bread. The Confederate troops had cornbread, which was hard and often moldy.

Reading
Passages

A Soldier's Life *(cont.)*

Weapons

Most soldiers used rifled muskets, which were loaded from the muzzle. The grooves inside the barrel helped the bullets travel farther and more accurately than the muskets used in earlier wars.

Skilled soldiers could fire three bullets a minute, but training was inconsistent, and many soldiers were poor marksmen. Soldiers behind fortified positions—using ditches, rocks, trees, and fences for protection—had a distinct advantage firing at attacking troops.

Artillery

Cannons played a major role in battles, too. Exploding cannon shells helped break up attacks by charging troops or blasted defensive positions. Cannon and gun smoke also created a thick haze, which made the battles even more chaotic and often led to soldiers being accidentally shot by their own troops.

As the war entered its final year, improvements in weaponry resulted in some Northern troops having repeating rifles that fired seven shots before reloading and breech-loading rifles that were much more accurate. The Gatling machine gun was put into use just as the war was winding down.

Left on the Field

Ambulance workers often carried soldiers to the surgeons' tents only after a battle was over, which meant that many soldiers spent the entire day lying helpless on the field. In the early years of the war, there was no system for removing the wounded, and some soldiers spent days and nights on the battlefield. Clara Barton and other volunteers gradually helped establish a system for removing soldiers from the battlefield. She and other volunteers worked while the battle itself was raging.

A Soldier's Life *(cont.)*

Illness

For every soldier killed in battle, four died of sickness or disease. Tens of thousands of soldiers were sickened by poor food and infection.

Most soldiers were generally unaware of the dangers caused by contagious diseases, bacteria, or illnesses carried by insects. Soldiers often had no source of clean water, especially in combat, and did not realize that drinking dirty water was likely to cause diseases such as typhoid fever or cholera.

Contagious Diseases

Many of the farm boys had never been exposed to measles, mumps, or chicken pox. These and other contagious diseases spread rapidly. The filth from so many men living in cramped quarters spread even more illnesses. Garbage, human waste, animal manure, and bloody bandages littered the camps. In addition, many soldiers never bathed.

Swamps had millions of mosquitoes carrying malaria and other disease-carrying insects. Lice and fleas were everywhere in most army camps, and almost every soldier was infested with them. In some units, dysentery and diarrhea affected 995 out of every 1,000 men. All these illnesses weakened soldiers, reduced their ability to fight, and made them more likely to catch other diseases. Soldiers would have suffered in even greater numbers if both the North and the South had not had voluntary sanitation committees, often led by determined women who insisted on bringing supplies, order, and cleanliness to the army camps.

Medicine

Both armies suffered from severe shortages of doctors, nurses, medicine, and hospitals. Most doctors only had two years of very simple medical training. They lacked medical knowledge and still believed in bleeding patients with pneumonia and some other diseases, a practice that had no positive effects and only weakened the patients more. The correlation between dirt and disease was little understood, which led to infection, amputation, and even death.

 Reading Passages

A Soldier's Life *(cont.)*

Amputation

The standard weapon used by soldiers during the Civil War was a rifle musket. The Minie bullet fired from these muskets destroyed so much tissue and bone when a soldier was hit that amputation was often the only chance for survival.

Cannon fire often tore off arms and legs and ripped jagged holes in the soldiers. To prevent death from blood poisoning and gangrene, surgeons used saws and meat cleavers to cut off arms and legs. Gruesome piles of limbs were stacked near a surgeon's headquarters after every battle.

No effort at cleanliness was attempted. Knives and saws were not even cleaned after each patient. Wounds and amputated stumps were rarely disinfected, and sometimes bandages were in such short supply that they were reused if a soldier died. Doctors were in such a hurry that they probed for bullets with their fingers, and wounds sometimes had cloth and filth caught in them.

Prisoners of War

Neither government expected the huge number of captured and wounded enemy prisoners. Neither the North nor South had any system in place for holding captured prisoners. They converted any available space into prisons—factories, warehouses, jails, schools, and abandoned forts. Prisoners, often weakened already by wounds, were often mistreated by guards. Food supplies were irregular and even more disgusting than regular army food.

About 56,000 soldiers in both armies died from the brutal conditions of these overcrowded, makeshift prisons. In the Southern prison at Andersonville, Georgia, at least 13,000 Union prisoners died from starvation, disease, and mistreatment. Prisoners had no clean water, were poorly clothed, and packed so closely together that they could barely move. Soldiers watched their friends suffer and die every day in this prison.

Reading Passages

Reconstruction

Restoring Order

After the surrender at Appomattox, the difficult process of restoring peace began. The assassination of Abraham Lincoln deeply affected what might have become a healing time. Lincoln was committed to the quick readmission of the seceded states and was concerned for their welfare and the welfare of freed slaves. With his death the powerful, radical Republican congressional leaders were determined to impose severe punishments upon the South and to ensure opportunities for the freed blacks.

The 10-year period after the war is referred to as Reconstruction because these radical congressional leaders wanted to change the South, both politically and economically. The war had created hundreds of thousands of veterans, many who were wounded and unable to care for themselves. Thousands of soldiers were still missing and unaccounted for.

Federal and state governments were simply overwhelmed by the damages the war had done to the South. Thousands of citizens had lost everything they owned.

About four million former slaves were now free but had little opportunity for jobs or any hope of providing for their families. The disruptions of the war had left many Southerners homeless and unable to provide for themselves, and the returning Confederate soldiers often had nothing to return to.

The Southern economy had to face many changes. There was a total absence of money which had any value. Farms and businesses had been destroyed. The plantation economy, based on slavery, was ended. These changes and the presence of an occupying force of federal troops placed the Southern economy and society in total disarray.

Elections

Federal troops and officials supervised elections, and some corruption and electoral fraud resulted. Southern whites feared and distrusted the newly freed slaves, and their supporters from the North angered Southern citizens.

Many Southerners tried to follow the advice of General Lee who told his soldiers to go home, plant crops, and be good citizens. But racism, violent hatred, and despair often overcame good intentions. Blacks found themselves unwanted, both in the South and in the North where many went trying to get jobs. They discovered that plenty of Northerners were racists, too.

Reading Passages

Reconstruction *(cont.)*

The Right to Vote

The 13th, 14th, and 15th Amendments to the Constitution were passed to provide newly freed blacks with liberties and the right to vote. During the Reconstruction period, many freed black men were able to vote. Some were elected to Congress, in fact, but this ended when the Reconstruction period ended. After the 10-year period of Reconstruction, blacks were effectively barred from voting and holding elective office, despite Constitutional protections.

It would take 100 years and the passage of the 1964 Voting Rights Act before Southern blacks would be able to exercise their constitutional rights. The final removal of federal troops from the South came as a result of an election bargain in 1876 when Democrats accepted the disputed election of Rutherford B. Hayes in exchange for the end of federal control in the South.

Ku Klux Klan

Some radical Southerners began intimidating and controlling black citizens with the creation of the Ku Klux Klan. The Klan and other local vigilante groups frightened, threatened, and killed blacks they felt were not sufficiently meek and obedient. Klansmen wore robes to disguise their identities and protect themselves from the law. These night riders went about shooting, hanging, whipping, and terrorizing blacks who sought to exercise their newly won freedom as well as any whites who were perceived as supporting the blacks.

Klansmen invaded prisons and lynched black prisoners, burned homes, tarred and feathered political enemies, murdered opponents, and used violence and force to affect elections. The Klan often visited and tried to frighten Northerners who had moved South to provide education for the mostly illiterate black population. Klan members greatly feared schools for blacks. Nathan Bedford Forrest, the Confederate cavalry hero who helped create and lead the Klan, actually turned against the organization when its members became increasingly violent, and he attempted to disband it.

Freedmen's Bureau

Just as the war ended, the federal government established the Freedmen's Bureau to help provide both blacks and whites with food, clothing, and some basic supplies to survive the post-war economic ruin in the South. The bureau often found itself trying to help both former slaves and slave owners as well as poor, white farmers. The Freedmen's Bureau was also very involved in teaching former slaves and their children to read.

Reading Passages

Reconstruction *(cont.)*

Carpetbaggers and Scalawags

Northern businessmen, political appointees, and federal officers who went South to enforce the authority of the federal government or to make money at the expense of the defeated Confederates were called *carpetbaggers* because many carried everything they owned in a cheap piece of luggage made from carpet pieces. Southerners who cooperated with Northern officials or went into business with carpetbaggers were called *scalawags*, a word suggesting they were cheats, small-time crooks, and traitors to their people.

The Impeachment of President Johnson

Lincoln had intended a two-way approach to Southern Reconstruction. He wanted to heal Southern wounds and treat the defeated people with dignity and respect. He also wanted to support the hopes of newly freed blacks.

Andrew Johnson, the vice president who succeeded Lincoln as president, was a Tennessee Democrat who supported the Union, but he did not have many allies in the government. He lacked the political skills and healing attitude of Lincoln. Some Congressional leaders felt Johnson was too soft on the defeated South and accused him of wrongdoing. They came within a single vote of removing him from office because he opposed their harsh

measures.

President Ulysses S. Grant

The election of General Ulysses S. Grant to the presidency calmed the political infighting which had infected Washington. It provided some measure of security to people in the defeated Southern states, but efforts to reconstruct the South, change its attitude toward the freed blacks, and become a more open society were doomed to failure.

Southern Leaders

Many Southern generals, officers, and political leaders followed General Lee's example and returned home to take up their lives again. Some started businesses and tried to help the Southern economy rebuild. Some—like General James Longstreet and John Singleton Mosby—actually joined the Republican Party, supported President Grant, and served in appointed government positions.

Other leaders refused all dealings with the North and were forbidden to run for either state or federal office by the occupying authorities who had to approve candidates for public offices. This led to greater resentment of the freed blacks and of the Southerners who associated with Northern officials. Reconstruction was not a long-term success.

Causes of the Civil War Quiz

Directions: Read pages 7–11 about the causes of the Civil War in the United States. Answer each question below by circling the correct answer.

1. Which invention made the cultivation of cotton profitable and led to large plantations with many slave laborers?
   a. printing press
   b. cotton gin
   c. railroad
   d. grain mill

2. Who wrote *Uncle Tom's Cabin?*
   a. Abraham Lincoln
   b. John C. Calhoun
   c. Louisa May Alcott
   d. Harriet Beecher Stowe

3. Which law required citizens to return runaway slaves to their owners?
   a. Fugitive Slave law
   b. Kansas-Nebraska Act
   c. Dred Scott decision
   d. Underground Railroad

4. Which of these people was not an abolitionist?
   a. Wendell Philips
   b. Frederick Douglass
   c. William Lloyd Garrison
   d. Stephen A. Douglas

5. Which abolitionist led an attack on Harpers Ferry and called for a slave rebellion?
   a. Frederick Douglass
   b. Abraham Lincoln
   c. John Brown
   d. William Lloyd Garrison

6. Which "conductor" of the Underground Railroad led more than 400 slaves to freedom?
   a. Abraham Lincoln
   b. Wendell Phillips
   c. Harriet Tubman
   d. Harriet Beecher Stowe

7. How many black slaves lived in the South when the Civil War began?
   a. 4 million
   b. 5 million
   c. 22 million
   d. 40 million

8. Who believed that a state could refuse to obey a law it did not like?
   a. Abraham Lincoln
   b. John C. Calhoun
   c. Andrew Jackson
   d. Henry Clay

9. An *abolitionist* is a person who
   a. supports slavery
   b. opposes war
   c. opposes slavery
   d. supports states' rights

10. Which state became a battleground between pro-slavery and anti-slavery forces?
    a. Kansas
    b. Nebraska
    c. New York
    d. Virginia

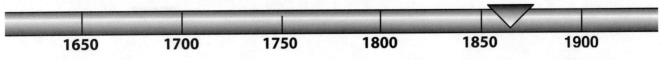
Civil War Leaders from the North Quiz

Directions: Read pages 12–14 about Northern leaders in the Civil War. Answer each question below by circling the correct answer.

1. Which Northern general was a great army organizer but not anxious to commit it to battle?
   a. Ulysses S. Grant
   b. George McClellan
   c. William Tecumseh Sherman
   d. John Brown

2. Which Northern leader became president of the United States in 1861?
   a. Ulysses S. Grant
   b. George McClellan
   c. Abraham Lincoln
   d. Frederick Douglass

3. Who stated that "war is all hell"?
   a. Abraham Lincoln
   b. William Tecumseh Sherman
   c. Ulysses S. Grant
   d. Philip Sheridan

4. Who was a black leader who wanted full civil rights for former slaves?
   a. Frederick Douglass
   b. George McClellan
   c. Philip Sheridan
   d. John Brown

5. Who ran for president of the United States as the Democratic candidate in 1864?
   a. Ulysses S. Grant
   b. George McClellan
   c. Abraham Lincoln
   d. Frederick Douglass

6. Which victory signaled the end of the Confederacy and helped Abraham Lincoln win reelection?
   a. Vicksburg
   b. Fort Sumter
   c. Atlanta
   d. Fort Donelson

7. Who was called the "Angel of the Battlefield"?
   a. Clara Barton
   b. John Brown
   c. William Tecumseh Sherman
   d. Dorothea Dix

8. Who attacked a government weapons storehouse at Harpers Ferry in 1859?
   a. Ulysses S. Grant
   b. John Brown
   c. Philip Sheridan
   d. Frederick Douglass

9. Who became the commander in chief of all Union armies after his victory at Vicksburg?
   a. Ulysses S. Grant
   b. George McClellan
   c. William Tecumseh Sherman
   d. Philip Sheridan

10. Which general had been a failure at everything before the war?
    a. Abraham Lincoln
    b. Ulysses S. Grant
    c. William Tecumseh Sherman
    d. Philip Sheridan

Civil War Leaders from the South Quiz

Directions: Read pages 15–17 about the Confederate leaders in the Civil War. Answer each question below by circling the correct answer.

1. Who was president of the Confederate States of America?
   a. Robert E. Lee
   b. Abraham Lincoln
   c. Jefferson Davis
   d. Stonewall Jackson

2. What military leader stood like a stone wall at the First Battle of Bull Run?
   a. Robert E. Lee
   b. Nathan Bedford Forrest
   c. Thomas Jackson
   d. John Hunt Morgan

3. Which officer once divided his men and had them charge both ways when surrounded by Union troops?
   a. John Singleton Mosby
   b. Nathan Bedford Forrest
   c. James Longstreet
   d. John Hunt Morgan

4. Which Confederate soldier was cautious and wanted to use a defensive strategy at Gettysburg?
   a. Robert E. Lee
   b. Nathan Bedford Forrest
   c. James Longstreet
   d. Stonewall Jackson

5. To whom did Abraham Lincoln first offer command of the Northern armies?
   a. Stonewall Jackson
   b. Robert E. Lee
   c. James Longstreet
   d. Jefferson Davis

6. Which Confederate cavalry officer was called "The Gray Ghost"?
   a. John Singleton Mosby
   b. Nathan Bedford Forrest
   c. J.E.B. Stuart
   d. John Hunt Morgan

7. Who led raids against Union forces in Kentucky, Tennessee, Mississippi, Indiana, and Ohio?
   a. J.E.B. Stuart
   b. John Hunt Morgan
   c. John Singleton Mosby
   d. Nathan Bedford Forrest

8. Which Confederate leader had once been secretary of war and a U.S. senator?
   a. Robert E. Lee
   b. John Hunt Morgan
   c. James Longstreet
   d. Jefferson Davis

9. Which Confederate cavalry leader said that he got there "fustest with the mostest"?
   a. John Singleton Mosby
   b. Nathan Bedford Forrest
   c. John Hunt Morgan
   d. Jefferson Davis

10. How do soldiers in the cavalry fight?
   a. on foot
   b. with cannons
   c. on horseback
   d. on ships

Civil War Battles 1 Quiz

Directions: Read pages 18–20 about some of the major battles of the Civil War. Answer each question below by circling the correct answer.

1. Which Civil War battle was watched by women, children, Congressmen, reporters, and other civilians?
   a. First Battle of Bull Run
   b. Vicksburg
   c. Shiloh
   d. Antietam

2. Which battle was the first major Union victory of the war?
   a. Fredericksburg
   b. First Battle of Bull Run
   c. Fort Donelson
   d. For Sumter

3. Which was the first battle of the Civil War?
   a. Fort Sumter
   b. First Battle of Bull Run
   c. Fort Donelson
   d. Shiloh

4. What was the Confederate name for the Battle of Shiloh?
   a. First Manassas
   b. Pittsburg Landing
   c. Fredericksburg
   d. Sharpsburg

5. Which battle was the single bloodiest day of the war with over 23,000 casualties?
   a. First Battle of Bull Run
   b. Antietam
   c. Shiloh
   d. Fredericksburg

6. Which Union commander at Antietam directed a poorly planned and disorganized attack?
   a. General Ulysses Grant
   b. General Robert E. Lee
   c. General George McClellan
   d. General John Pope

7. Which ironclad ship fought the *Virginia* at Hampton Roads?
   a. *Merrimack*
   b. *Monitor*
   c. *Donelson*
   d. *Manassas*

8. Who ordered the bombardment of Fort Sumter?
   a. Abraham Lincoln
   b. Major Robert Anderson
   c. General Pierre Beauregard
   d. General Robert E. Lee

9. Which Union general had the nickname "Unconditional Surrender"?
   a. General Ulysses Grant
   b. General Ambrose Burnside
   c. General Robert E. Lee
   d. General George McClellan

10. Which of these battles was a Union victory?
    a. First Battle of Bull Run
    b. Shiloh
    c. Second Battle of Bull Run
    d. Fredericksburg

Civil War Battles 2 Quiz

Directions: Read pages 21–23 about some of the major battles of the Civil War. Answer each question below by circling the correct answer.

1. Which Union victory helped lead to the reelection of President Lincoln?
   a. Cold Harbor
   b. Atlanta
   c. Gettysburg
   d. Petersburg

2. In what battle did Union forces overcome strong Confederate resistance, capture Missionary Ridge, and win a victory?
   a. Chickamauga
   b. Spotsylvania
   c. Gettysburg
   d. Chattanooga

3. In which battle was Stonewall Jackson mortally wounded?
   a. Chancellorsville
   b. Petersburg
   c. Gettysburg
   d. Chickamauga

4. Who commanded the Confederate army at Chickamauga?
   a. Ulysses S. Grant
   b. Robert E. Lee
   c. William Rosecrans
   d. Braxton Bragg

5. Which word means "to surround a city or fort to force its surrender"?
   a. artillery
   b. siege
   c. cavalry
   d. casualties

6. Which Union general marched his troops from Atlanta to Savannah in 1864?
   a. William T. Sherman
   b. Ulysses S. Grant
   c. William Rosecrans
   d. Joseph Hooker

7. Which battle occurred when Robert E. Lee marched troops into Pennsylvania to try to force an end to the war?
   a. Vicksburg
   b. Chancellorsville
   c. Gettysburg
   d. Petersburg

8. Which Union victory gave the North control of the Mississippi River?
   a. Chickamauga
   b. Cold Harbor
   c. Atlanta
   d. Vicksburg

9. Which successful siege left Richmond open to capture by Union forces?
   a. Atlanta
   b. Petersburg
   c. The Wilderness
   d. Vicksburg

10. Where did Lee surrender to Grant?
    a. Petersburg
    b. Cold Harbor
    c. Gettysburg
    d. Appomattox

A Soldier's Life Quiz

Directions: Read pages 24–29 about soldiers' lives during the Civil War. Answer each question below by circling the correct answer.

1. What was the median age of soldiers in the Civil War?
   a. 18
   b. 24
   c. 3
   d. 45

2. How many soldiers died in prisoner of war camps?
   a. 13,000
   b. 25,000
   c. 56,000
   d. 1,000

3. What did the Union soldiers call "teeth dullers" and "sheet-iron crackers"?
   a. hardtack biscuits
   b. beans
   c. dried beef
   d. cornbread

4. How many black soldiers served in the union army?
   a. 56,000
   b. 180,000
   c. 13,000
   d. 1,000

5. Which group of soldiers often worked as water boys, barbers, cooks, and surgeon's assistants?
   a. Native Americans
   b. farm boys
   c. drummer boys
   d. prisoners of war

6. How could wealthy Northern men avoid the draft?
   a. own 20 slaves
   b. pay a substitute
   c. own a farm
   d. go to college

7. What percent of the Northern troops were born in foreign countries?
   a. 50 percent
   b. 9 percent
   c. 18 percent
   d. 25 percent

8. What did sanitation committees do?
   a. fix rifles
   b. provide cleanliness and supplies
   c. help surgeons operate
   d. drill soldiers

9. Which of these is not a disease which affected Civil War soldiers?
   a. lice
   b. typhoid
   c. chicken pox
   d. cholera

10. Which of these was not a reason so many arms and legs were amputated during the Civil War?
    a. rifled muskets
    b. cannon fire
    c. Minie bullets
    d. land mines

Reconstruction Quiz

Directions: Read pages 30–32 about the Reconstruction era after the Civil War. Answer each question below by circling the correct answer.

1. What organization was created in the South to threaten freed slaves and their supporters?
   a. Ku Klux Klan
   b. Underground Railroad
   c. Scalawags
   d. Congress

2. Which president was impeached and nearly removed from office?
   a. Abraham Lincoln
   b. Rutherford B. Hayes
   c. Ulysses S. Grant
   d. Andrew Johnson

3. Who advised Confederate soldiers to go home, plant crops, and be good citizens?
   a. Jefferson Davis
   b. Robert E. Lee
   c. Nathan Bedford Forrest
   d. Ku Klux Klan

4. What term did Southerners use to describe Northerners who tried to make money at the expense of the defeated South?
   a. carpetbaggers
   b. scalawags
   c. Congressmen
   d. Freedmen

5. Who wanted to heal Southern wounds and help freed slaves achieve success?
   a. Radical Republicans
   b. President Johnson
   c. President Lincoln
   d. Ku Klux Klan

6. Which Southern leader supported President Grant, joined the Republican Party, and held an appointed position?
   a. Robert E. Lee
   b. James Longstreet
   c. Rutherford B. Hayes
   d. Jefferson Davis

7. What name did Southerners call other Southerners who cooperated with Northern officials and businessmen?
   a. scalawags
   b. carpetbaggers
   c. Confederates
   d. Ku Klux Klan

8. Who tried to remove President Johnson from office?
   a. Ku Klux Klan
   b. President Grant
   c. congressmen
   d. carpetbaggers

9. Which Americans were supposed to be helped by the 13th, 14th, and 15th amendments to the Constitution?
   a. businessmen
   b. freed slaves
   c. Union soldiers
   d. Confederate soldiers

10. Who supervised elections in the South during Reconstruction?
   a. General Lee
   b. Ku Klux Klan
   c. Abraham Lincoln
   d. federal officials

Teacher Lesson Plans for Language Arts

Vocabulary, Newspapers, and Letter Writing

Objectives: Students will learn to apply their language arts skills to vocabulary enrichment, finding information in newspapers, and writing friendly letters.

Materials: copies of Civil War Vocabulary (page 43); newspapers; copies of Read All About It (page 44); copies of Writing Home (page 45)

Procedure

1. Reproduce and distribute Civil War Vocabulary (page 43). Review the vocabulary and pronunciation if necessary. Have students complete the page independently.

2. Distribute copies of newspapers. Reproduce and distribute Read All About It (page 44). Review the sections in a newspaper, and have students complete the activity sheet.

3. Reproduce and distribute Writing Home (page 45). Review the assignment and the format of a friendly letter. Tell students to use their background reading to help write the letters.

Assessment: Correct the vocabulary work sheet together. Have students share their newspaper entries in small groups or with the class. Allow students to share their letters with the class.

Poetry

Objective: Students will develop skills in reading and understanding poetry.

Materials: copies of Reading Poetry in Two Voices (page 46); copies of "Barbara Fritchie" (pages 47 and 48); copies of Figurative Language in "Barbara Fritchie" (page 49); copies of Narrative Poetry in Two Voices (page 50) and copies of poems listed on the page; copies of Focus on Poets (page 51); poems by Walt Whitman and John Greenleaf Whittier (available in books and on the Internet)

Procedure

1. Reproduce and distribute Reading Poetry in Two Voices (page 46) and "Barbara Fritchie" (pages 47 and 48). Have students review the vocabulary and rhyme in the poem.

2. Review reading poetry in two voices, stressing the importance of timing so that the two voices work in unison. You may wish to assign this activity to two capable students and have them demonstrate how to present a narrative poem.

3. Reproduce and distribute Figurative Language in "Barbara Fritchie" (page 49). Review the figurative language in the poem "Barbara Fritchie."

4. Reproduce and distribute the Narrative Poetry in Two Voices (page 50). Have each student pair choose a poem or song listed on page 50, or assign one. Tell them to divide it into two parts with a chorus, and allow them to practice it together for several days before presenting it to the class. Help them with unfamiliar words and terms.

5. Reproduce and distribute the Focus on Two Poets (page 51). Assign poems by Walt Whitman and John Greenleaf Whittier to each team of students. Tell them to look for the poem's message, describe any figurative language, and define vocabulary.

Assessment: Have students present their poems to the entire class. Base performance assessments on pacing, volume, expression, and focus of the participants.

Teacher Lesson Plans for Language Arts *(cont.)*

Literature

Objective: Students will read and respond to a variety of fictional accounts of the Civil War.

Materials: copies of *Mine Eyes Have Seen* (pages 52 and 53); copies of Focus on Author Ann Rinaldi (page 54); copies of Elements of a Novel (page 55); copies of Civil War Diaries (pages 56 and 57); copies of *Nightjohn* and *Sarny* (page 58); copies of the books *Mine Eyes Have Seen, Nightjohn, Sarny,* and others listed on page 54; copies of diaries listed on page 56

Procedure

1. Reproduce and distribute *Mine Eyes Have Seen* (pages 52 and 53). Depending on the number of available books, assign the books to an individual, a group, or the class. Have students complete the comprehension questions (page 52) and also share their responses to the What Do You Think? questions (page 53). Assign the Response to Literature (page 53), and have students write a four-paragraph essay about the book *Mine Eyes Have Seen*. Review the structure of the essay as given on the page.

2. Reproduce and distribute the Focus on Author Ann Rinaldi (page 54) and Elements of a Novel (page 55) activity pages. Help students choose appropriate novels. Review the Elements of a Novel work sheet. Instruct students to complete the story outline for the novels they chose. When finished, allow individual students to share with the class, especially their personal evaluation of the books they read.

3. Reproduce and distribute Civil War Diaries (page 56 and 57). Assign the diaries to an individual, a group, or the class, depending on the number of books available. Many public libraries have these popular series. Instruct students to complete the diary notes evaluation. Have them start their own personal diary or journal. Students can use a small, bound notebook or staple some pages together and add a cover to make their own. Encourage students to make entries each day for two or more weeks.

4. Reproduce and distribute the *Nightjohn* and *Sarny* activity sheet (page 58). Have as many students as possible read one or both of these books. Instruct students to answer the questions independently. Then discuss the questions as a class to stimulate student understanding and interest about slavery in the United States during this time period. Ask students which book they thought was more interesting, and have them give specific reasons for their opinions.

Assessment: Use student activity pages and class discussions to assess students' performance on the literature selections.

Teacher Lesson Plans for Language Arts *(cont.)*

Speeches

Objective: Students will develop oral presentation techniques and skills in public speaking.

Materials: copies of Lincoln's Gettysburg Address (pages 59 and 60); copies of Great Speeches (page 61); copies of famous speeches listed on page 61 (available in books and on the Internet)

Procedures

1. Reproduce and distribute Lincoln's Gettysburg Address (pages 59 and 60). Review the vocabulary with students. Read the speech to the class, or have a student do so. Explain the importance of stressing powerful, significant words in a speech. Have students underline important words in the Gettysburg Address. Review the tips for giving a speech on page 60. Challenge students to memorize the speech and deliver it to the class or students in another class.

2. Reproduce and distribute Great Speeches (page 61). Have students select a famous speech or a portion of one to deliver. Use books and the Internet for sources. Assist students to edit longer speeches by choosing significant parts of it. Allow them to use note cards when giving the speech, but tell them that they are not to just read the speech. Schedule time for students to practice and then deliver their speeches. Have students analyze the speech they chose, using the questions on page 61.

Assessment: Critique students' delivery of the speeches to the class. Assess their understanding of the speeches by reviewing their answers to the Analyzing the Speech work sheet.

Readers' Theater

Objective: Students will learn to use their voices effectively in dramatic reading.

Materials: copies of Readers' Theater Notes (page 62); copies of Readers' Theater: The Defense of Little Round Top (pages 63 and 64)

Procedure

1. Reproduce and distribute Readers' Theater Notes (page 62). Review the basic concepts of Readers' Theater with the class.

2. Reproduce and distribute Readers' Theater: The Defense of Little Round Top (pages 63 and 64). Put students in small groups, and allow time over several days for them to practice reading the script together.

3. Schedule class performances, and have students share the prepared script.

4. Use the suggestions in the Extension activity at the bottom of page 62 to allow students to write their own Readers' Theatre. Assign topics to teams of students, or let them choose their own. Allow time for them to create and practice their scripts.

5. Schedule classroom performances of these scripts, or invite another class to view the production.

Assessment: Base performance assessments on pacing, volume, expression, and focus of the participants. Student-created scripts should demonstrate appropriate writing skills, dramatic tension, and a good plot.

Civil War Vocabulary

Directions: Match each word in Column 1 with its correct meaning in Column 2. Use a dictionary, the glossary at the end of the book, and student-reading pages to help find these words related to the Civil War.

Column 1

_____ 1. **Confederate**

_____ 2. **artillery**

_____ 3. **cavalry**

_____ 4. **ironclad**

_____ 5. **scalawags**

_____ 6. **carpetbaggers**

_____ 7. **Reconstruction**

_____ 8. **plantation**

_____ 9. **inauguration**

_____ 10. **blockade**

_____ 11. **territory**

Column 2

a. a ship covered with iron plates

b. soldiers fighting on horseback

c. Southerners who cooperated with Union officials after the war

d. swearing-in of a president

e. a large farm with one or two cash crops

f. land which is not yet a state

g. Northerners who went South to profit from the South's defeat

h. the recovery period in the South after the Civil War

i. using ships to block the ports of a city

j. cannons and other explosives

k. states which left the Union

Directions: Fill in the missing words from the list below to complete each of the following sentences.

Word List

| arsenal | infantry | musket | secede |
| casualties | ironclad | rebels | sentry |

12. The _____ in South Carolina decided to _____ from the Union.

13. An _____ soldier carried a _____ into battle.

14. Cannons and ammunition were kept in the _____ at Harpers Ferry.

15. A _____ walked his post for four hours.

16. Large, _____ warships inflicted many _____ in battle.

Read All About It

During the Civil War, people on both sides of the conflict received most of their information from newspapers. Newspapers carried accounts of the war as well as interviews with soldiers and reporters who were there. Long lists of casualties were published after each battle, and some battlefield photographs were even printed. The Civil War was the first war in which the public had immediate information about events. Despite the influence of television and modern communication today, newspapers still provide detailed and wide-ranging information about daily life.

Directions: Read an article from the following sections in a current newspaper. On the lines below, write a headline and a brief summary of the article. Be prepared to share your findings with the class.

Name of Newspaper: _____

National or World News

 Headline: _____

 Summary: _____

 _____

State or Local News

 Headline: _____

 Summary: _____

 _____

Editorials/Opinion

 Headline: _____

 Summary: _____

 _____

Sports

 Headline: _____

 Summary: _____

 _____

Directions: Write what is found in the following sections of a newspaper, and find an example of each.

Classifieds _____

Comics _____

Obituaries _____

Real Estate _____

Writing Home

Soldiers on both sides of the Civil War wrote letters home to their families and loved ones. In these letters they expressed their feelings about the cause they were fighting for, their homesickness, what they were experiencing as soldiers, and sometimes their fears as they prepared for battle. Many even predicted their own deaths in an upcoming battle. The love letters written to wives and girlfriends expressed the soldiers' deep emotions. Soldiers were especially eager to receive letters from home, too.

Directions: Do either Assignment 1 or 2 below. Use this book or any Civil War nonfiction book, diary, or novel you have read for ideas, facts, and information. *Behind the Blue and Gray: The Soldier's Life in the Civil War* by Delia Ray is especially good.

Assignment 1

Imagine you are a soldier fighting in the Civil War or a nurse working in a battlefield hospital. Write a letter to a friend, your parents, a loved one, or a neighbor. Describe some of the difficulties you have encountered, a battle you were in, life in the army, the behavior of your officers, the food, medical treatment, your travels, illnesses, or general conditions in your military unit.

Assignment 2

Imagine you are a friend, parent, loved one, or neighbor of a soldier fighting on either side of the Civil War. Write a letter to that soldier. Tell him what is happening at home with his family, relate hometown news, describe local efforts to support the war, express your feelings about the war, and mention any political and social events. Use the correct format for a friendly letter as shown below.

_____
(Date)

Dear _____,

_____

_____

_____

Sincerely yours,

_____
(Signature)

Reading Poetry in Two Voices

Directions: The poem "Barbara Fritchie" (pages 48 and 49) has been arranged to be read aloud by two readers. Read the introduction to the poem on the next page, and then read the entire poem silently to yourself several times. Check the meanings of words and phrases in the poem as noted below. Choose a partner to work with, and decide who will be the first and second reader. Read the chorus parts together. Practice reading the poem aloud several times over the course of a week or so. Present your dramatic reading to the class or to students in another class.

Poetic Words and Phrases

bier—framework for a coffin

clustered spires—church steeples in a group

famished—starved

fourscore years and ten—ninety years

gash—deep cut

host—army

o'er—over

rebel horde—massed Confederate soldiers

rebel tread—the march of the Confederate soldiers

rent—tore

royal will—proud

silken scarf—flag

silver stars . . . crimson bars—symbols on the confederate flag

slouched—tipped to one side

staff—flagpole

tost—tossed; flew

yon—over there

Assignment

Poets often use rhyming words at the end of lines in poetry to achieve a pleasing effect and to highlight some aspect of the poem, such as the marching in "Barbara Fritchie." Highlight or underline the last words of each line in the poem, and then answer the following questions.

1. What pattern did you find? _____

    _____

2. Does every ending word in a couplet (a pair of lines) have a rhyming partner? _____

1650 | 1700 | 1750 | 1800 | 1850 | 1900

"Barbara Fritchie"

In early September of 1862, General Stonewall Jackson's troops were marching through the town of Frederick in central Maryland. People in this town and state were deeply divided over the war. According to some accounts, a 96-year-old Union patriot named Barbara Fritchie flew an American flag from her upstairs window which was shot at by Confederate soldiers. She grabbed the flag and waved it, telling the Confederate soldiers to shoot her rather than the flag. John Greenleaf Whittier heard about the incident and memorialized the story in this poem.

First Speaker

"Barbara Fritchie"

By John Greenleaf Whittier

Second Speaker

Up from the meadows rich with corn,

Clear in the cool September morn,

The clustered spires of Frederick stand

Green-walled by the hills of Maryland.

First Speaker

Round about them orchards sweep,

Apple and peach trees fruited deep,

Fair as the garden of the Lord

To the eyes of the famished rebel horde,

Second Speaker

On the pleasant morn of the early fall

When Lee marched over the mountain-wall;

Over the mountains winding down,

Horse and foot, into Frederick town.

Chorus

Forty flags with their silver stars,

Forty flags with their crimson bars,

Flapped in the morning wind; the sun

Of noon looked down, and saw not one.

First Speaker

Up rose old Barbara Fritchie then,

Bowed with her fourscore years and ten;

Bravest of all in Frederick town,

She took up the flag the men hauled down;

Second Speaker

In her attic window the staff she set,

To show that one heart was loyal yet.

Up the street came the rebel tread,

Stonewall Jackson riding ahead.

© *Teacher Created Resources, Inc.*47#3214 Civil War

"Barbara Fritchie" *(cont.)*

Chorus

Under his slouched hat left and right
He glanced; the old flag met his sight.
"Halt!" the dust-brown ranks stood fast,
"Fire!" out blazed the rifle-blast.

First Speaker

It shivered the window, pane and sash;
It rent the banner with seam and gash.
Quick, as it fell, from the broken staff
Dame Barbara snatched the silken scarf.

Second Speaker

She leaned far out on the window-sill,
And shook it forth with a royal will.

Chorus

"Shoot, if you must, this old gray head,
But spare your country's flag," she said.

Second Speaker

A shade of sadness, a blush of shame,
Over the face of the leader came;
The nobler nature within him stirred
To life at that woman's deed and word;

Chorus

"Who touches a hair of yon gray head
Dies like a dog! March on!" he said.

First Speaker

All day long that free flag tost
Over the heads of the rebel host.
Ever its torn folds rose and fell
On the loyal winds that loved it well;

Second Speaker

And through the hill-gaps sunset light
shone over it with a warm goodnight.
Barbara Fritchie's work is o'er,
and the Rebel rides on his raids no more.

First Speaker

Honor to her! And let a tear
Fall, for her sake, on Stonewall's bier.

Chorus

Over Barbara Fritchie's grave,
Flag of Freedom and Union, wave!
Peace and order and beauty draw
Round thy symbol of light and law;
And ever the stars above look down
On thy stars below in Frederick town!

Figurative Language in "Barbara Fritchie"

Poets use figurative language to paint word pictures for the reader and the listener. *Personification, simile,* and *metaphor* are three types of figurative language used in the poem "Barbara Fritchie" (pages 47 and 48).

Personification

Personification is a technique used to make something that is not human act or feel like a person.

> "And ever the stars above look down
>
> On thy stars below in Frederick town!"

The stars are portrayed as living creatures looking down on the flags in the town of Frederick.

Metaphor

A *metaphor* is a comparison in which one thing is spoken of as if it was another.

> "And shook it forth with a royal will."

Barbara's determination is compared to the will of a king or queen.

Simile

A *simile* is a comparison of two different things using the words "like," "as," or "than."

> "Fair as the garden of the Lord."

The Maryland countryside is compared to the Garden of Eden, where Adam and Eve lived.

Assignment

Find and discuss the following examples of figurative language in the poem "Barbara Fritchie."

1. Personification:
   - "Ever its torn folds rose . . ."
   - "the sun / Of noon . . ."
   - "and through the hill-gaps sunset light . . ."
   - "Peace and order and beauty . . ."
2. Metaphors:
   - "Up from the meadows . . ."
   - "Bowed with her . . ."
3. Simile:
   - "Dies like a . . ."

Narrative Poetry in Two Voices

Reading poetry aloud with a friend is another way to enjoy it. With this type of presentation, two or more students recite a poem together, alternating verses or stanzas and even reading some lines together. Use the poem "Barbara Fritchie" (pages 47 and 48) as an example for dividing your own poem into parts. This technique can be used with any poem and also with some songs, but it is especially effective with story poems and ballads.

Assignment

Choose a partner, and then select a poem or song from the lists below or one your teacher provides. Pick one that appeals to you because of the rhyme, rhythm, or subject matter. Then divide the poem or song into parts so that you and your partner can narrate it together. Choose at least a few lines that both of you will recite together. Make a copy so that each of you has one to work with. Practice together so that you have the same speed, volume, and pace. Highlight or underline words that should receive special emphasis. Try to get a feel for the mood and flow of the poetic language. Practice the poem or song several times over the course of a week or more, and then recite it for your class.

Suggested Poems

An Old-Time Sea Fight by Walt Whitman
Annabel Lee by Edgar Allan Poe
The Ballad of the Oysterman by Oliver Wendell Holmes
The Bells by Edgar Allan Poe
Casey at the Bat by Ernest Lawrence Thayer
Casey Jones (author unknown)
The Charge of the Light Brigade by Alfred Lord Tennyson
The Cremation of Sam McGee by Robert W. Service
The Death of King Arthur by Alfred Lord Tennyson
Eldorado by Edgar Allan Poe
The Highwayman by Alfred Noyes
John Henry (author unknown)
Lochinvar by Sir Walter Scott
O Captain! My Captain! by Walt Whitman
Ode to Billy Joe by Bobbie Gentry
Paul Revere's Ride by Henry Wadsworth Longfellow
The Skeleton in Armor by Henry Wadsworth Longfellow
The Walrus and the Carpenter by Lewis Carroll

Civil War Songs

Try these Civil War songs in two voices without music.

"The Battle Hymn of the Republic"
"Dixie"
"Goober Peas"
"We're Tenting Tonight on the Old Campground"
"When Johnny Comes Marching Home"

| 1650 | 1700 | 1750 | 1800 | 1850 | 1900 |

Focus on Poets

Two of the most admired poets of 19th century America were Walt Whitman and John Greenleaf Whittier. Both lived long lives and were involved in public affairs and especially in the events leading up to and during the Civil War.

Walt Whitman

Born in 1819 on Long Island, New York, Whitman grew up in Brooklyn. He worked as a schoolteacher, a printer, and a journalist as well as being an aspiring poet. Whitman was intensely interested in public affairs and political activities. He enjoyed mixing with people of every social background and took the opportunity to talk to people at every opportunity. He even rode ferries and stagecoaches just for the conversational opportunities. During the Civil War, Whitman was a government clerk in Washington, DC. He spent a lot of time during the war as a volunteer nurse's aide in military hospitals.

Whitman's poetry celebrated the ideal of democracy and the idea that the United States had a crucial role to play in leading the world toward peace, harmony, and freedom. His most famous poems were a collection called *Leaves of Grass*. He wrote a collection of Civil War poetry called *Drum Taps*, which included "Pioneers! O Pioneers!" and "Beat! Beat! Drums!" He wrote two poems about the death of President Abraham Lincoln: "When Lilacs Last in the Dooryard Bloom'd" and "O Captain! My Captain!" He died in 1892.

John Greenleaf Whittier

John Greenleaf Whittier was born in 1807 to a family of Quaker farmers in Haverhill, Massachusetts. Throughout his life, the influence of his religion was evident in his poetry and his politics. Whittier became a committed abolitionist in his 20s and worked as a Massachusetts legislator and as a newspaper writer to convince the nation that slavery was morally wrong. His poems often carried an anti-slavery message.

Whittier was opposed to any compromise with the Southern states that led to the return of fugitive slaves or which allowed slavery to continue to exist. He supported the Union cause during the Civil War as is evident in his poem "Barbara Fritchie" (pages 48 and 49). Whittier also wrote many poems celebrating New England life and culture. Some of his more famous poems include "Ichabod," "Snow-Bound," "Telling the Bees," "The Hunters of Men," "The Slave Ships," and "Skipper Ireson's Ride." Like Walt Whitman, he died in 1892 after a long and productive life.

Assignment

Read a poem by Walt Whitman or John Greenleaf Whittier. Look for the figurative language within the poem. (See page 49 for examples of figurative language.) Determine the central message of the poem. Read the poem to the class, and describe the poem's meaning.

Mine Eyes Have Seen

Annie Brown is the 15-year-old girl who narrates *Mine Eyes Have Seen*, an adventure story set just before the Civil War. Annie's father, John Brown, was one of the most eccentric and extraordinary men of his time. As a young man, he became a committed enemy of slavery and spoke frequently about its evils. Brown held many jobs, owned farms and businesses, and was generally unsuccessful in everything. A deeply religious man, Brown framed many of his abolitionist activities in the language of a religious crusade.

In Kansas, John Brown became a hero to abolitionists and a terror to proslavery forces. He led violent raids against the Missouri factions who had raided anti-slavery towns in Kansas. His militant skirmishes angered people in both states where fighting had already erupted in the late 1850s.

Mine Eyes Have Seen details the summer Annie spent with her father in Maryland as he gathered men and weapons for his attack on the United States arsenal at Harpers Ferry, Virginia. The purpose of the raid was to start a slave revolt and rebellion in the Southern states. Through Annie's eyes, we see the unstable character of her father, the type of people he recruited in his war on slavery, and the shattering impact the raid had on her life and the nation.

Assignment

Read *Mine Eyes Have Seen* by Ann Rinaldi, and answer the comprehension questions below.

1. Who did Annie Brown fall in love with?_____

2. How many men did John Brown have with him when he attacked Harpers Ferry?_____

3. Which of Brown's sons was his most important aide? _____

4. Why did Frederick Douglass refuse to join in the attack on Harpers Ferry? _____

   _____

5. Which two men gave Annie the most trouble about staying hidden?_____

   _____

6. Which of Annie's brothers refused to join their father on his last raid?_____

7. What nosy neighbor did Annie make friends with? _____

8. What incident happened when Annie was young that her father always blamed her for?_____

   _____

9. What happened to Hettie Pease? _____

   _____

10. What happened to John Brown after the raid? _____

   _____

| 1650 | 1700 | 1750 | 1800 | 1850 | 1900 |

Mine Eyes Have Seen (cont.)

What Do You Think?

Discuss the following questions in small groups or with the entire class.

1. Was John Brown justified in using force to attack slavery?

2. Should Annie have tried to talk Dauphin out of going with her father?

3. Was Annie really responsible for her sister Amelia's death?

4. Was John Brown a good father? Explain your reasons, giving specific examples from the story.

5. Which of the men in the company did you most admire? Why?

6. Why does Annie feel uncomfortable at Orchard House in Concord?

7. Why did the men choose to follow John Brown?

8. What would you have done if John Brown had asked you to join him?

9. Was Frederick Douglass right not to join Brown's crusade?

10. Who was the most important member of John Brown's raiding party? Give your reasons.

Response to Literature

Write an essay giving your understanding and impressions of the book *Mine Eyes Have Seen.* The essay should include the following elements:

Paragraph 1

Describe Annie Brown's character and personality. Mention her strong character traits, and list instances from the book which illustrate her courage, determination, perseverance, and other traits. Describe your personal feelings about Annie.

Paragraph 2

Describe the character and personality of John Brown. Use examples of things he did to show his stubborness, courage, determination, and miscalculations. Describe your attitude toward John Brown as a leader and as a father.

Paragraph 3

Would you have followed John Brown on his missions? Give several reasons and incidents from the book to support your decision.

Paragraph 4

Give your personal impressions of the book *Mine Eyes Have Seen.*

Focus on Author Ann Rinaldi

Ann Rinaldi is one of the most effective authors of historical fiction for young readers. Her novels are especially appealing to readers who like determined, headstrong, confident, young heroines. Rinaldi's books are painstakingly accurate in detail and filled with the small details of life which create a sharp edge of reality in her writing. Her novels are based on the lives of real individuals and have interesting and important characters who actually lived during an historical period. Rinaldi says her interest in writing historical fiction was sparked by her son Ron who "turned her on to history" and loaned her many books from his library.

Other Books by Ann Rinaldi

A Break With Charity: A Story About the Salem Witch Trials. Harcourt, 1992. (A narrative about an unwilling participant in the witch trials)

Hang a Thousand Trees with Ribbons: The Story of Phillis Wheatley. Harcourt, 1996. (A novel based on the life of the talented slave poet)

The Last Silk Dress. Holiday House, 1988. (The story of a Confederate girl trying to help the Cause who comes face-to-face with the darker side of her way of life)

Numbering All the Bones. Hyperion, 2002. (An extraordinary Civil War novel set near the infamous Southern prison at Andersonville)

A Ride into Morning: The Story of Tempe Wick. Harcourt, 1991. (A novel of the American Revolution)

The Second Bend in the River. Scholastic, 1997. (The story of a young girl's love for a Native American leader)

The Secret of Sarah Revere. Harcourt, 1995. (A story of the American Revolution)

Taking Liberty: The Story of Oney Judge, George Washington's Runaway Slave. Simon & Schuster, 2002. (An account of a favorite "servant" to the Washingtons)

Time Enough For Drums. Random House, 1986. (A Revolutionary War story)

Wolf by the Ears. Scholastic, 1991. (The story of Harriet Hemings, daughter of Sally Hemings and Thomas Jefferson, who must choose whether to escape from slavery)

Other Civil War Novels

Beatty, Patricia. *Who Comes with Cannons?* Scholastic, 1992. (Excellent story of a Quaker girl caught in the conflict over slavery and war)

Hunt, Irene. *Across Five Aprils.* Berkley, 1964. (Classic Newbery Honor winner about a boy who comes of age in the Civil War)

Paulsen, Gary. *Nightjohn.* Dell, 1993. (See page 58.)

Paulsen, Gary. *Sarny.* Delcorte, 1997. (See page 58.)

Reit, Seymour. *Behind Rebel Lines: The Incredible Story of Emma Edmonds, Civil War Spy.* Harcourt, 2001. (Slightly fictionalized account of the exploits of a Civil War soldier)

Elements of a Novel

Assignment

Read a book by Ann Rinaldi or one of the Civil War novels listed on page 54. Complete the outline below. Then share the information with a small group or the entire class.

Story Outline

Book Title: _____

Genre (historical fiction, fantasy, contemporary realism): _____

Setting of the story (where and when): _____

Protagonist (one or two facts about the central character): _____

Major characters (include one or two descriptive facts about each): _____

_____

Lesser characters (include one or two descriptive facts about each): _____

_____

Point of view (Is the story told in first person or third person?): _____

Plot (3–6 sentences about the story line): _____

_____

_____

_____

_____

Problem/Conflict (basic problem in one sentence): _____

_____

Climax (story's turning point): _____

_____

Resolution (how the story ends): _____

_____

Feeling/Tone (book's general tone—depressing, uplifting, sad, funny, etc.): _____

Theme (ideas the story addresses, such as good versus evil): _____

_____

Personal evaluation (your response to the characters and story): _____

_____

_____

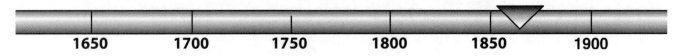

| 1650 | 1700 | 1750 | 1800 | 1850 | 1900 |

Civil War Diaries

Many soldiers in the Civil War kept diaries and journals in which they detailed their experiences during the war. They recorded the battles, camp conditions, and events of their lives. The Civil War also produced a rich harvest of civilian journals and diaries kept by people who were profoundly affected by the war. The list below includes two actual diaries and several fictional ones based on real events.

True Diaries

Sateren, Shelley Swanson, ed. *A Civil War Drummer Boy: The Diary of William Bircher 1861–1865.* Blue Earth Books, 2000. (Fascinating diary of a Northern drummer boy who served throughout the war)

Steele, Christy and Anne Todd, eds. *A Confederate Girl: The Diary of Carrie Berry, 1864.* Blue Earth Books, 2000. (Interesting diary of a Confederate girl in 1864)

Fictional Diaries

Denenberg, Barry. *When Will This Cruel War Be Over? The Civil War Diary of Emma Simpson.* Dear American Series, Scholastic, 1996. (Exceptionally well-written diary of a Virginia girl whose life is being destroyed by the war as the North invades her part of the country)

Duey, Kathleen. *Emma Eileen Grove: Mississippi, 1865.* American Diaries, Aladdin, 2000. (Events in the life of a girl in Mississippi who is caught up in the chaos of post-war life)

Duey, Kathleen. *Maddie Retta Lauren: Georgia, 1864.* American Diaries, Aladdin, 2000. (The story of a Georgia girl caught in Sherman's March to the Sea)

Hansen, Joyce. *I Thought My Soul Would Rise and Fly: The Diary of Patsy, a Freed Girl.* Dear America Series, Scholastic, 1997. (The diary of a black girl in 1865 who taught herself to read and write and is now experiencing freedom)

McKissack, Patricia C. *A Picture of Freedom: The Diary of Clotee, a Slave Girl.* Dear America Series, Scholastic 1997. (The diary of a slave who decides to escape to freedom along the Underground Railroad)

Osborne, Mary Pope. *My Brother's Keeper: Virginia's Diary.* My America Series, Scholastic, 2000. (The diary of a Pennsylvania girl at Gettysburg as the battle begins)

Civil War Diaries *(cont.)*

Assignment

Read one of the diaries described on the previous page. There are numerous books in the *Dear America, My America*, and *American Diaries* series, and many are set during the Civil War. Complete the evaluation below, giving specific examples from the diary you read. Share your observations with a small group or the entire class.

Diary Notes

Title of Diary: _____

Writer's Personal Data (age, personality, character traits, hopes and desires): _____

Setting (where and when): _____

_____

Problem (circumstances, situations, conflicts): _____

_____

Important Characters in the Diary (friends, enemies, neighbors): _____

_____

Events (Describe one interesting and one sad event): _____

_____

Impressions (Describe your thoughts about the book and writer.): _____

_____

_____

Create Your Own Diary

Start your own diary or journal today. Try to record at least one entry each day. Include some of the following:

- Describe important events that are happening in your personal life.
- Mention events in the world or your community which are affecting your life or may do so in the future.
- Tell about important people in your life.
- Describe books you are reading which influence your thinking.
- Share some of your dreams and hopes for the future.

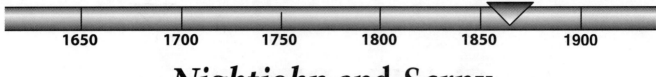
Nightjohn and Sarny

Nightjohn

Gary Paulsen wrote two extraordinary pieces of historical fiction set in the Civil War era. *Nightjohn* is the story of a 12-year-old slave girl on a Southern plantation who is secretly taught how to read by an older slave named Nightjohn. Teaching slaves to read was strictly prohibited in most Southern states because the owners feared that it would encourage slaves either to run away or to revolt. This book offers the reader a clear view of the harsh realities of slave life.

Assignment

Read *Nightjohn*. Then answer the following questions on a separate sheet of paper.

1. Why did Sarny not know her own mother?

2. How did Waller know Sarny was learning to read?

3. How did Nightjohn teach Sarny and others to read?

4. What does Sarny mean when she says it is wrong to run from slavery?

5. What happened to Jim, Pawley, and Alice when they ran? Which runner was treated the worst?

6. Why did Nightjohn admit he taught Sarny?

7. Why do you think Waller treated his slaves so badly?

8. What were the punishments for learning to read according to Nightjohn?

9. Why do you think the book is dedicated to Sally Hemings?

10. What was Nightjohn's punishment?

11. How did Sarny know that Nightjohn had returned?

12. Why did Nightjohn return?

Sarny

Sarny is the sequel to *Nightjohn*. It relates Sarny's perils and adventures as she tries to find her two children, who have been sold to a slave trader. Caught in the violence and disruption of the Civil War, Sarny and her friend set out through the chaos of war and journey all the way to New Orleans, meeting some very interesting people on the way.

Assignment

Read *Sarny*. Then answer the following questions on a separate sheet of paper.

1. Who is Miss Laura and why is she able to help Sarny?

2. Why is Sarny worried about Lucy?

3. How did Miss Laura manage to be so successful, despite her color?

4. Why did Sarny's school get burned?

5. Why was Stanley killed?

1650   1700   1750   1800   1850   1900

Lincoln's Gettysburg Address

The speech U.S. President Abraham Lincoln made on November 19, 1863, at the Gettysburg battlefield lasted only a little over two minutes. It followed a speech by a famous orator who had spoken for almost two hours. Lincoln felt that his speech was a failure, as did some newspapers. However, it soon came to be regarded as one of the greatest speeches ever written. Although the address is only 269 words long, it contains 10 powerful sentences.

Assignment

Review the meanings of the words listed below. Then read the Gettysburg Address. Underline the most important words, and read Lincoln's speech again.

abolish—to end or do away with

conceive—to create an idea

consecrate—to make sacred

engaged—working together

Founding Fathers—the men who created the nation during the American Revolution

died in vain—die without success

fourscore—eighty (four times twenty)

hallow—to make holy or sacred

last full measure of devotion—their lives

proposition—plan, suggestion, idea

The Gettysburg Address

"Fourscore and seven years ago our fathers brought forth on this continent a new nation, conceived in liberty and dedicated to the proposition that all men are created equal.

Now we are engaged in a great civil war, testing whether that nation or any nation so conceived and so dedicated can long endure. We are met on a great battlefield of that war. We have come to dedicate a portion of that field as a final resting place for those who here gave their lives that that nation might live. It is altogether fitting and proper that we should do this.

But, in a larger sense, we cannot dedicate—we cannot consecrate—we cannot hallow—this ground. The brave men, living and dead, who struggled here, have consecrated it, far above our poor power to add or detract. The world will very little note, nor long remember, what we say here, but it can never forget what they did here.

It is for us the living, rather, to be dedicated here to the unfinished work which they who fought here have thus far so nobly advanced. It is rather for us to be here dedicated to the great task remaining before us—that from these honored dead we take increased devotion to that cause for which they gave the last full measure of devotion—that we here highly resolve that these dead shall not have died in vain—that this nation, under God, shall have a new birth of freedom—that government of the people, by the people, for the people, shall not perish from the earth."

Lincoln's Gettysburg Address *(cont.)*

Challenge

Memorize the entire Gettysburg Address on the previous page. There are only 10 sentences. Then give the speech to the class or a small group. Emphasize significant verbs, nouns, and adjectives when giving the speech. Do not stress words like *a, before, cannot, for,* or *the*. Refer to the suggestions listed below to help you prepare.

Giving a Speech

Below are some things to keep in mind when delivering a speech or giving a talk in front of others.

❏ **Memorize**

Memorize what you are going to say instead of just reading word for word. Write the speech in large letters on index cards, and refer to your notes only when necessary.

❏ **Use Good Posture**

Stand up straight. Relax your body, and be comfortable.

❏ **Use Eye Contact**

Look at various sections of the audience as you speak but not at any one person in particular.

❏ **Rehearse Out Loud**

Practice giving your speech out loud in front of a mirror or to a friend, a sibling, or adult family members. Do this several times.

❏ **Breathe From Your Diaphragm**

Take deep breaths between sentences and important points, but do not be obvious about it. (The diaphragm is the large muscle at the bottom of your rib cage which allows you to control your breathing.)

❏ **Speak Slowly, Clearly, and with Volume**

Speak a little slower than normal. Pronounce each word clearly so your audience can hear what you are saying. Speak loudly enough for everyone to hear, but do not shout. Vary your voice pattern to emphasize words, phrases, and ideas.

❏ **Enjoy the Experience**

Public speaking is a great accomplishment. Relax and enjoy the opportunity.

Great Speeches

Choose one of the famous speeches listed below. Use the Internet, a book, or encyclopedia to find a copy of it. Memorize a part of the speech or the entire speech if it is less than five minutes long. Try to get the tone and emphasis that the original speaker might have used. If desired, wear clothing from the time period when the speech was given. Then deliver the speech to the class.

Famous Speeches

Abraham Lincoln's first inaugural address

Abraham Lincoln's second inaugural address

Daniel Webster's Bunker Hill oration

Franklin D. Roosevelt's first inaugural address

George Washington's Farewell Address

John Kennedy's second inaugural address

Martin Luther King's "I Have a Dream" speech

Patrick Henry's "Give Me Liberty or Give Me Death" oration

The Preamble and Declaration of Rights from The Declaration of Independence

Ronald Reagan's Challenger disaster speech

Seneca Falls Convention's "Declaration of the Rights of Women"

Sojourner Truth's "Ain't I a Woman?" speech

Winston Churchill's Iron Curtain speech

Analyzing the Speech

Directions: Answer the following questions about the speech you selected.

1. What speech did you choose? _____

2. Who gave the speech originally? _____

3. On what date was the speech given? _____

4. To whom was the speech given? _____

5. Which words were unfamiliar to you? What do they mean in this context?

Words	Meanings
_____	_____
_____	_____
_____	_____
_____	_____

6. What was the speaker's purpose in giving the speech? Who was the speaker trying to influence?

_____

_____

7. What was the main idea of the speech? _____

_____

_____

Readers' Theater Notes

Readers' Theater is drama that does not require the use of costumes, props, stage, or memorization. It is done in the classroom by groups of students who become the cast of the dramatic reading.

Staging

Place four or five stools, chairs, or desks in a semicircle at the front of the class or in a separate staging area. Generally no costumes are used in this type of dramatization, but students dressed in similar clothing or colors can add a nice effect. Simple props can be used but are not required.

Scripting

Each member of your group should have a clearly marked script. Performers should practice several times before presenting the play to the class.

Performing

Performers should enter the classroom quietly and seriously. They should sit silently without moving and wait with their heads lowered. The first reader should begin, and the other readers should focus on whoever is reading, except when they are performing.

Assignment

Read the Readers' Theater script (pages 63 and 64) about the assault of Little Round Top at the Battle of Gettysburg. Work with your group to prepare for the performance, and share your interpretation of the script with the class.

Extension

Write your own Readers' Theater script based on one of the events listed below or another topic related to the Civil War period. Practice your script with a group of classmates, and then perform it for the rest of the class.

- A slave decides to run away from his or her owner.

- John Brown prepares to attack Harpers Ferry.

- General Lee surrenders to Grant at Gettysburg.

- Abraham Lincoln prepares the Gettysburg Address.

- Abraham Lincoln and his cabinet debate the Emancipation Proclamation.

- Lincoln is assassinated at Ford's Theater.

- A soldier prepares for battle at Shiloh, Antietam, or another battle.

- Clara Barton prepares to help soldiers during a battle.

Readers' Theater: The Defense of Little Round Top

This script is an account of the assault on Little Round Top, an important hilltop, during the second day of the Battle of Gettysburg and its defense by a beleaguered regiment, the 20th Maine volunteers and their extraordinary commander, Colonel Joshua Lawrence Chamberlain. There are six speaking parts.

Narrator: The time is late afternoon on July 2, 1863, at the climatic Battle of Gettysburg. A small, beleaguered, and outnumbered regiment of about 320 Northern soldiers—the 20th Maine—is holding the crucial heights on Little Round Top, a hill overlooking part of the battlefield. They are at the very end of the Union lines. If the attacking Alabama forces can outflank them or push them off the hill, then the entire Union army is at risk of being overrun and destroyed by the armies of General Robert E. Lee. The commander of the 20th Maine, Colonel Joshua Lawrence Chamberlain, is a former professor of philosophy, foreign language, and history from tiny Bowdoin College in Maine.

First Soldier: Boys, we are in a fix. It looks like half the Rebel army out there is getting ready to charge up this hill. I do not see how we can hold out.

Second Soldier: They are coming up on our weak side to the left, too. This is going to be a rough one, boys.

First Soldier: I do not know what to think of our colonel either. He is not a regular officer, you know. He was a college professor before the war.

Corporal: Well, he has done fine so far. After all, none of us were soldiers before the war.

First Soldier: But he taught literature and poetry and philosophy. What does he know about war? These Southern officers will outsmart him for sure.

Sergeant: They are getting ready to charge. Our biggest problem is that we are short of ammunition, and nobody can get any to us. We are totally cut off.

Narrator: Colonel Chamberlain joins his soldiers to explain the situation and his plan.

Colonel Chamberlain: Men, listen well. The enemy intends to turn our flank. If we lose the left flank, they will take this hill and command the heights for their final assault on Gettysburg tomorrow. Every soldier knows it is essential to hold the high ground.

Readers' Theater: The Defense of Little Round Top *(cont.)*

Second Soldier: They have got us pretty badly outnumbered, Colonel, maybe more than two to one. On top of that, we are just about out of ammunition, and we have no artillery support. How are we going to hold them off?

Colonel Chamberlain: We are going to use a military tactic I learned while teaching Greek history. It was used in a Greek war thousands of years ago. Be prepared to move forward at my command. Hurry, men, we have no time to lose. The enemy is advancing.

First Soldier: I hope the colonel knows what he is doing. If he does not, we are going to end up as Confederate mincemeat.

Sergeant: Form up, men! We have no time to waste. Ready! Here they come!

Colonel Chamberlain: Stand firm, ye boys of Maine, for not once in a century are men permitted to bear such responsibilities for freedom and justice, for God and humanity as are placed upon you.

Corporal: Ready! Aim! Fire!

Reload! Fire!

Reload! Fire!

Fire at will!

Second Soldier: We are out of bullets. We have used up everything we have! What will we do, Colonel?

Sergeant: We are trapped in the open. We have got only two choices—advance or retreat—and we have no bullets left!

Colonel Chamberlain: If we retreat here, the Union could lose the war. Retreat is out of the question. Gentlemen, fix bayonets!

Corporal: Fix bayonets! Charge!

Charge bayonets! Attack! Attack!

Narrator: The men of the 20th Maine charged down the hill against their attackers. Their bayonet charge eventually swept the Confederate forces back, and survivors of the 20th Maine regiment held Little Round Top. The Union army did win at Gettysburg. Colonel Chamberlain was seriously wounded in six separate battles and twice reported dead on the battlefield. However, he survived to accept the surrender of one Confederate army at the end of the war. He returned home to teach at Bowdoin College, where at one time or another he taught every subject except math.

Teacher Lesson Plans for Social Studies

Using Time Lines

Objectives: Students will learn to derive information from a time line and make time lines relevant to them.

Materials: copies of the Civil War Time Line (pages 67 and 68); reference materials including books, encyclopedias, texts, atlases, almanacs, and Internet sites

Procedure

1. Collect available resources so that students have plenty of materials in which to find information.

2. Review the concept of a time line, using events from the current school year as an example.

3. Reproduce and distribute the Civil War Time Line (pages 67 and 68). Review the various events listed on the time line.

4. Instruct students to place additional dates on the time line as described in the assignment on page 68.

5. Encourage students to research the dates of events listed in the Challenge section and to find nine additional ones to include on their time lines.

Assessment: Verify the accuracy of the dates and events that students added to the time line. Assess students' ability to research other events to add to it.

Using Maps

Objective: Students will learn to use and derive information from maps.

Materials: copies of Union and Confederate States (page 69); copies of Important Civil War Battles (page 70); atlases, almanacs, and other maps for reference

Procedure

1. Review the map on Union and Confederate States (page 69), and make sure that students are able to read the map key. Ask students to identify the eight territories that had not yet become states. Assign the map activity on the page.

2. Review Important Civil War Battles (page 70). Have students use the information on the map to complete the activity. Discuss the Extension question at the bottom of the page. (Students might indicate that many battles were fought in Virginia and Tennessee because Virginia was an important political and economic center and Tennessee blocked major routes into the heartland of the Confederacy.)

Assessment: Correct the map activities together. Check for understanding and review basic concepts as needed.

Teacher Lesson Plans for Social Studies *(cont.)*

Researching the Civil War

Objectives: Students will develop skills in finding, organizing, and presenting research information.

Materials: copies of Researching Civil War Battles (page 71); copies of Become a Civil War Hero or Heroine (pages 72 and 73); copies of Famous People of the Civil War (page 74); books, encyclopedias, and Internet sources

Procedure

1. Review the information on Researching Civil War Battles (page 71). Stress the need to take notes in an organized manner, the information required for each battle, and potential sources to use. Assign a battle to each student. Remind students to use their own words and to proofread for spelling, punctuation, and other writing conventions.

2. Review the information on Become a Civil War Hero or Heroine (pages 72 and 73). Discuss the outline on page 73 and the need to take notes to help prepare for the presentation.

3. Allow students to select the person from the list on page 74 who they wish to portray. Remind students that they need to find a lot of information about their heroes. Point out that at least 400 women fought in disguise as male soldiers during the Civil War.

4. Give students time to research their person and prepare their dramatic presentations. Arrange a schedule so students can share with the class.

Assessment: Assess students on the basis of their written reports on the battles. For students' oral presentations as famous people, use the following categories and grading percentages, or create a rubric of your choosing:

General Knowledge (50%)

Dramatic Skill (10%)

Vocal Presentation (Loud/Clear) 20%

Costume (10%)

Notes (10%)

Civil War Time Line

1859

Oct. 16 – John Brown and 21 followers begin occupation of Harpers Ferry and call for a slave uprising.

Dec. 2 – John Brown is hanged for treason.

1860

Nov. 6 – Abraham Lincoln is elected U.S. president.

Dec. 2 – South Carolina secedes from the Union.

1861

Jan. 9 – Mississippi secedes from the Union.

Jan. 10 – Florida secedes.

Jan. 11 – Alabama secedes.

Jan. 19 – Georgia secedes.

Jan. 21 – Five Southern senators, including Jefferson Davis, resign from the United States Senate.

Jan. 26 – Louisiana secedes.

Jan. 29 – Kansas becomes the 34th state, a free state opposed to slavery.

Feb. 1 – Texas secedes.

Feb. 9 – Jefferson Davis is elected president of the Confederacy.

Mar. 4 – Abraham Lincoln is inaugurated as the 16th president of the U.S.

Mar. 6 – Davis calls for 100,000 volunteer troops.

Apr. 12 – Confederate troops fire on Fort Sumter, and war begins.

Apr. 13 – Fort Sumter surrenders to Confederate forces.

Apr. 15 – President Lincoln calls for 75,000 Union volunteer troops.

Apr. 19 – Lincoln orders a blockade of Southern ports.

Apr. 20 – Robert E. Lee resigns from the U.S. Army.

May 6 – Arkansas secedes.

May 7 – Tennessee secedes.

May 20 – North Carolina secedes.

May 21 – Richmond, Virginia, becomes the capital of the Confederate states.

May 23 – Virginia secedes.

July 21 – The South wins the First Battle of Bull Run (Manassas).

Nov. 1 – George B. McClellan becomes the Union commander in chief.

1862

Feb. 16 – General Grant wins a major victory at Fort Donelson.

Mar. 9 – The first battle occurs between ironclad warships, the *Monitor* and the *Merrimack*. Neither wins.

Apr. 7 – Grant defeats Confederate forces at Shiloh with heavy losses on both sides.

Apr. 16 – Slavery is abolished in Washington, DC.

Apr. 25 – The Union navy captures New Orleans, Louisiana.

May 4 – Union troops capture Yorktown and move toward Richmond.

June 1 – Lee assumes command of the Army of Northern Virginia.

July 1 – Lee's troops save Richmond in a seven-day battle.

Aug. 4 – Lincoln calls for 300,000 soldiers.

Aug. 30 – Lee and Jackson lead the South to victory in the Second Battle of Bull Run.

Sept. 17 – Northern forces win the Battle of Antietam at Sharpsburg, Maryland, in the single bloodiest day of fighting in the war.

Civil War Time Line *(cont.)*

1863

Jan. 1 – Lincoln issues the Emancipation Proclamation.

Mar. 3 – The Union passes a law to draft soldiers.

July 3 – The Battle of Gettysburg ends in a Northern victory.

July 4 – Grant's siege of Vicksburg ends in a Southern defeat.

Nov. 19 – Lincoln delivers the Gettysburg Address.

1864

Mar. 9 – Ulysses S. Grant becomes commander in chief of Union forces.

June 3 – Battle of Cold Harbor costs heavy Union casualties.

June 20 – Grant begins siege of Petersburg, VA.

Sept. 2 – Sherman's troops capture Atlanta.

Nov. 8 – Lincoln is reelected president of the U.S.

Nov. 15 – Sherman begins his march through Georgia.

Dec. 21 – Sherman's troops take Savannah, GA.

1865

Apr. 2 – Confederate troops abandon Petersburg and Richmond, VA.

Apr. 9 – Lee surrenders to Grant at Appomattox.

Apr. 14 – Lincoln is assassinated in Washington, DC.

Apr. 15 – Andrew Johnson is sworn in as president of the U.S.

May 26 – The last Confederate troops surrender.

Dec. 24 – The Ku Klux Klan is formed in Mississippi to stop efforts to give civil rights to free blacks.

1867

July 19 – The last of three Reconstruction Acts is passed to admit Confederate states back into the Union.

1868

Nov. 3 – Ulysses S. Grant is elected president of the U.S.

1877

Apr. 24 – The last federal troops leave the South, and Reconstruction is officially over.

Assignment

Study the time line above. Add the following Civil War battles to the time line. Use the Internet, textbooks, encyclopedias, almanacs, and other sources to find the dates.

- Chancellorsville
- Chattanooga
- Chickamauga
- Fort Henry
- Fredericksburg
- Kennesaw Mountain
- Mobile Bay
- Murfreesboro
- Nashville
- Seven Days
- Spotsylvania
- Wilderness

Challenge

Find the dates of the following events, and add them to the time line. Find nine additional events that occurred between 1850 and 1876, and include those also.

- Comstock Lode silver strike is made.
- Dred Scott Decision is handed down.
- Lincoln proclaims a national day of Thanksgiving.
- Transcontinental railroad is completed.
- *Uncle Tom's Cabin* is published.
- West Virginia splits from Virginia and becomes a state.

Union and Confederate States

Directions: Use the map below to list the 23 states that remained loyal to the Union and the 11 that seceded to form the Confederate States of America.

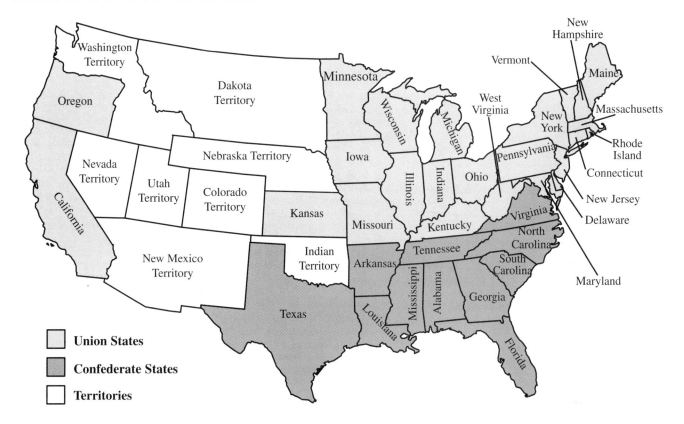

Union States

1. _____
2. _____
3. _____
4. _____
5. _____
6. _____
7. _____
8. _____
9. _____
10. _____
11. _____
12. _____

13. _____
14. _____
15. _____
16. _____
17. _____
18. _____
19. _____
20. _____
21. _____
22. _____
23. _____

Confederate States

1. _____
2. _____
3. _____
4. _____
5. _____
6. _____
7. _____
8. _____
9. _____
10. _____
11. _____

Important Civil War Battles

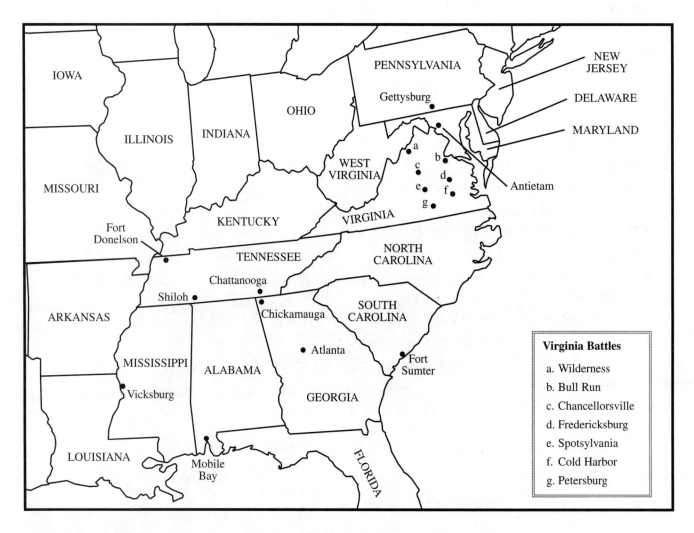

Virginia Battles

a. Wilderness

b. Bull Run

c. Chancellorsville

d. Fredericksburg

e. Spotsylvania

f. Cold Harbor

g. Petersburg

Directions: The above map shows the location of some of the major Civil War battles. On a separate sheet of paper, write the battles fought in each state. The number in parentheses indicates how many battles to list. Then use a colored pencil to shade in the Confederate States.

1. Alabama (1)
2. Georgia (2)
3. Maryland (1)
4. Mississippi (1)
5. Pennsylvania (1)
6. South Carolina (1)
7. Tennessee (3)
8. Virginia (7)

Extension

Why do you think so many battles were fought in Virginia and Tennessee?

_____

_____

_____

1650 1700 1750 1800 1850 1900

Researching Civil War Battles

Assignment

Research at least one Civil War battle. Take notes before writing a first draft. Find the following information about the battle.

- Date of the battle
- Place of the battle (city, town, state, river, etc.)
- Length of the battle in days
- Generals in charge of each army
- Important leaders involved in the actual battle
- Numbers of fighting men on each side
- Problems faced by the Union
- Problems faced by the Confederates
- Weapons used by each side
- Special acts of bravery during the battle (leading a charge, fighting against a vastly superior number, etc.)
- How the battle came about (What was each army trying to do?)
- The influence of weather and terrain on the battle
- Results of the battle (who won, effect on public sentiment)

Battles of the Civil War

Antietam (Sharpsburg)	Kennesaw Mountain
Atlanta	Malvern Hill
Chancellorsville	Mobile Bay
Chattanooga	*Monitor* and *Merrimack*
Chickamauga	Second Battle of Bull Run (Manassas)
Cold Harbor	Seven Days
Fair Oaks (Seven Pines)	Sherman's March to the Sea
First Battle of Bull Run (Manassas)	Shiloh (Pittsburg Landing)
Fort Donelson	Siege of Petersburg
Fort Henry	Siege of Vicksburg
Fort Sumter	Spotsylvania Court House
Fredericksburg	Stones River (Murfreesboro)
Gettysburg	Wilderness
Hampton Roads	

Challenge

Draw a map of the battle you researched. Show where each army began, and use arrows to indicate the direction of the fight. Include all the information that you can on the map.

©*Teacher Created Resources, Inc.*71*#3214 Civil War*

Become a Civil War Hero or Heroine

A great way to understand Civil War history is to become a Civil War hero or heroine. That way you become familiar not only with the person but also the time period in which he or she lived and how the issues of the day affected his or her life.

Do the Research

Use the guidelines on the next page to help plan your dramatic portrayal of a Civil War hero or heroine. Remember that you do not have to know every little detail about the person's life but should know the important information.

Be Prepared

Get a friend to quiz you about your person so that you learn what you need to study and are confident about what you already know. When other students are being questioned during their presentations, write down questions that you could not answer about your own character, and then look up the answers later.

Get in Costume

Put together an appropriate costume from clothing you have at home. Check your closets for pants, shirts, or old costumes that might work, and ask family members or friends for articles of clothing they could lend. Soldiers' uniforms varied enormously and were often dark blue, black, or gray depending upon what soldiers had available. Hats can often be shaped from construction paper or tagboard. If possible, wear leather shoes or boots since tennis shoes were not invented yet. Stuff them with tissue if they are too big. Use a prop that fits with your character. A sword for an officer and a book for a writer or politician are examples of effective props. First make sure the props are appropriate and allowed at school.

Stay in Character

Remember who you are portraying. You are a hero or heroine—not just a student. Be serious, and avoid silly behavior. At the end of questions from classmates, review the important facts about your life.

Be Dramatic

Speak clearly and loudly. Do not get nervous and rush through your presentation. Use your hands, arms, and prop to emphasize important points. Use facial and body gestures, and stride across the front of the room if appropriate. Take charge of the classroom. Have confidence in yourself.

Be Famous

One way to begin your presentation is to state, "My name is . . . . What would you like to know about me?" You might instead want to begin with a brief presentation, listing five or six important facts about your Civil War character. This will give your classmates a place to begin with their questions. Have a story to tell or something else to say if there is a momentary pause in the questioning.

Become a Civil War Hero or Heroine *(cont.)*

Assignment

Choose a Civil War hero or heroine you admire from the list on page 74, and use the outline below to help you research important information about that person. Use several resources (textbooks, almanacs, encyclopedias, the Internet, and other reference materials), and learn all you can about that person. Take notes on index cards, and then organize your presentation. Learn the important dates, vital statistics, and the achievements and struggles in his or her life. Try to assume the personality of your hero or heroine. Practice over and over until you are ready.

Biographical Outline

I. Youth

    A. Birthplace and date

    B. Home life and experiences

        1. Brothers and sisters

        2. Places lived (parts of the country, farm or town)

        3. Circumstances (rich or poor; important events)

    C. Schooling (When and how much?)

    D. Childhood heroes

    E. Interesting childhood facts and stories

II. Civil War Experiences

    A. Experiences during the war

        1. Which side he/she supported (Union or Confederate?)

        2. Battles participated in

        3. Dangers faced (give details)

    B. Lifestyle and personal habits

        1. Values and beliefs

        2. Personal qualities (cruel, kind, honest, etc.)

    C. Leadership experiences

        1. Jobs held

        2. Influential people in his/her life

        3. Significant events

    D. Successes and failures

        1. Contributions to the war effort

        2. Accomplishments

        3. Failures

        4. Greatest challenges

III. Death

    A. Date and place

    B. Age

    C. Cause

Famous People of the Civil War

Northerners

Abraham Lincoln—U.S. president who saved the Union

Andrew Johnson—president of the U.S. after Lincoln's death

Clara Barton—"Angel of the Battlefield"; founded the Red Cross

David Farragut—naval hero at Mobile Bay

Dorothea Dix—superintendent of nurses and soldiers' advocate

Dred Scott—slave in the landmark Supreme Court decision

Edward Everett—minister and orator who also spoke at Gettysburg

Elizabeth Van Lew—Southern foe of slavery and spy

Ely Parker—Iroquois general

"Fighting Joe" Hooker—courageous general

Frederick Douglass—a former slave who fought for freedom

George A. Custer—daring, controversial cavalry officer

George G. Meade—hot-tempered general

George McClellan—he could organize an army but did not fight

Harriet Beecher Stowe—antislavery author of *Uncle Tom's Cabin*

Harriet Tubman—helped slaves to freedom through the Underground Railroad

John Brown—radical abolitionist who lit the fuse of war

John Greenleaf Whittier—Quaker poet who supported the Union

Joshua Lawrence Chamberlain—school teacher hero at Gettysburg

Mary Livermore—helped create and fund sanitation committees

Mary Todd Lincoln—wife of Abraham Lincoln

Mathew Brady—photographer who brought the war home

Philip Sheridan—general who controlled the Shenandoah Valley

Sarah Emma Edmonds—soldier, spy, nurse

Stephen A. Douglas—a man of compromise and character

Ulysses S. Grant—a stubborn, unflappable warrior

Walt Whitman—abolitionist poet and Union supporter

William Lloyd Garrison—fierce advocate of abolition

William T. Sherman—he understood modern warfare

Southerners

A.P. Hill—much valued general to Lee and Jackson

Albert Sidney Johnson—Confederate hero of Shiloh

Belle Boyd—spied on Union officers

Braxton Bragg—general with few friends or admirers

George Pickett—led the most famous charge of the war

J.E.B. Stuart—dashing, but not always reliable cavalry officer

James Longstreet—Lee's "Old War Horse"

Jefferson Davis—president of the Confederacy

John Bell Hood—brave, almost reckless general

John Hunt Morgan—his raiders caused havoc among Union troops

John Wilkes Booth—actor who assassinated Lincoln

Joseph E. Johnston—tough but often defeated general

Jubal Early—aggressive, courageous commander

Mary Chesnut—her journal brings Southern feelings to life

Nathan Bedford Forrest—brilliant, eccentric, cavalry leader

P.T. Beauregard—a good general in a lost cause

Robert E. Lee—brilliant strategist who came close to victory

Thomas J. "Stonewall" Jackson—eccentric, brilliant general

Varina Davis—wife of Confederate President

Culminating Activities

Civil War Day

Set aside one day to be devoted to activities related to your study of the Civil War. If possible, do this with two or three classes at the same grade level. This allows you to share some of the responsibilities and provides a special experience for the entire grade level.

Parent Help

Encourage parents or adult family members to come for all or part of the day to enjoy the proceedings and to help set up and monitor the activities. Check with parents to discover any special talents, interests, or hobbies that would be a match for specific centers.

Costumes

Invite students to come in the period costumes they used in their research presentations on Civil War heroes and heroines (pages 72 and 73). Ask one or two parents to use makeup to provide boys with mustaches and beards to give a period look for the day. Many Civil War books offer useful illustrations.

Eat Hearty

If you have parent volunteers, plan a luncheon with a Civil War theme. Have students make table decorations at one of the centers. Make sure students do not have food allergies or any dietary restrictions.

Battle Reenactment

Have students use the information they learned from researching Civil War battles (page 71) to reenact a portion of a battle. Tell students that many people perform in these activities on actual Civil War battlefields. You will want to assign a role to each student and explain that you want them to try to be as historically accurate as possible. This could be done in a whole class reenactment or by groups in a center. As an alternative, you might want to show students part of *Gettysburg, Glory,* or another appropriate Civil War film.

Play Baseball

Baseball was the most popular sport for soldiers on both sides of the Civil War. The game was a little different then, however. There was no designated hitter, home runs were very rare, any ball hit among the spectators had to be returned, there were only wooden bats, and the stolen base was first used in 1863. Plan a game of baseball (or softball), possibly at the end of your special day.

Skates Away

The first patent for roller skates was awarded in 1863. Depending upon the weather and time of year, you might want to allow students to bring their skates to school and arrange a skating activity or contest. Make sure students wear the necessary safety gear such as helmets, knee pads, elbow pads, and wrist guards.

Culminating Activities *(cont.)*

Centers

The centers you set up should relate in some way to the Civil War, daily life during this period, or activities from this book. Centers should involve small groups of six or seven students doing an activity and/or making something they can display. Each center should take about 20 minutes after which time students should rotate to the next activity. The following are suggestions for various centers, or you may add others for which you have special expertise.

☐ **Discussion Center**

A center could be set up where students argue the pros and cons of Civil War events. Divide students into two groups to debate the issues from either the Confederate or Union position. Debates could focus on the reasons for secession, the rights of citizens, and conduct during war. Students can use the reading selections and research activities in this book for ideas and background information.

☐ **Poetry Center**

Each person in the poetry center would team with a partner and present one of the narrative poems studied in this book to an audience.

☐ **Readers' Theater**

This center would involve students practicing with a script for a Readers' Theater presentation. Students could use the script in this book or write their own.

☐ **Reconstruct a Civil War Battlefield or Map**

Students at this center would reconstruct a Civil War battlefield using modeling clay, scrap fabric pieces, construction paper, small sticks, and/or other craft materials. Students will need books or pictures of various battlefields to use for reference. A variety of battlefield maps could also be created in this center. Use the maps in this book for examples and find others in atlases, books, encyclopedias, and on the Internet. The maps can be drawn on tagboard or construction paper, or three-dimensional maps can be built using clay or salt and flour.

☐ **Clay Figures or Busts**

In this center, students can use modeling clay or blocks of inexpensive sculpting clay to make figures or busts of Civil War heroes and heroines they studied. A 25-pound bag of sculpting clay can be sliced into 18 or more rectangular blocks of clay with a piece of fish line. Provide craft sticks to carve the features. Have plenty of paper towels available for cleanup.

Annotated Bibliography

Nonfiction

Biel, Timothy Levi. *Life in the North During the Civil War.* Lucent, 1997. (Factual account of Northern lifestyle during the war)

Bolotin, Norman. *Civil War A to Z: A Young Reader's Guide to Over 100 People, Places, and Points of Importance.* Dutton, 2002. (Good source with lots of information)

Chang, Ina. *A Separate Battle: Women and the Civil War.* Scholastic, 1991. (Exceptional overview of the important roles women played in the war)

Collier, Christopher and James Lincoln Collier. *Reconstruction and the Rise of Jim Crow 1864–1896.* Cavendish, 2000. (Good middle-grade treatment of Reconstruction and its aftermath)

Cox, Clinton. *Undying Glory: The Story of the Massachusetts 54th Regiment.* Scholastic, 1991. (Very readable account of the first black regiment in the Civil War)

Freedman, Russell. *Lincoln: A Photobiography.* Scholastic, 1987. (Superb, Newbery Award-winning biography of Lincoln)

Hakim, Joy. *War, Terrible War.* Oxford University Press, 1994. (Exceptional basic account of the war with events and major players seen from interesting and enlightening perspectives)

McPherson, James M. *Fields of Fury: The American Civil War.* Atheneum, 2002. (Excellent accounts of the battles by a major Civil War historian)

Mettger, Zak. *Reconstruction: America After the Civil War.* Dutton, 1994. (Informative account of life during that troubled period)

Murphy, Jim. *The Long Road to Gettysburg.* Scholastic, 1992. (Outstanding account of the battle by one of the best historical writers)

Piggins, Carol Ann. *A Multicultural Portrait of the Civil War.* Cavendish, 1994. (An account of the lives and accomplishments of Native Americans, African Americans, and immigrants during the war)

Ray, Delia. *Behind the Blue and Gray: A Soldiers' Life in the Civil War.* Scholastic, 1991. (Excellent account for children of soldiers' lives on both sides of the war)

Sinnott, Susan. *Welcome to Addie's World 1864: Growing Up During America's Civil War.* American Girl, 1999. (Interesting facts about life for women and children during the war)

Stanchak, John. *Civil War.* Dorling Kindersley Eyewitness Books, 2000. (Great illustrations and facts)

Sterling, Dorothy. *The Story of Harriet Tubman: Freedom Train.* Scholastic, 1954. (Classic account of this great leader)

Poetry

Burns, Marjorie, ed. *The Charge of the Light Brigade and Other Story Poems.* Scholastic 1990. (Great compendium of ballads and story poems to use for poetry in two voices)

Burns, Marjorie, ed. *Casey at the Bat and Other Poems to Perform.* Scholastic, 1990. (Fun story poems to perform in class)

Glossary

abolitionist—a person opposed to slavery

agriculture—farming and raising crops

allies—people or nations on the same side of a war

arsenal—a place used to make and store weapons and ammunition

artillery—cannons and other high-powered explosives

bayonet—a long, steel blade attached to the barrel of a rifle

blockade—the use of ships to surround a port and prevent goods from being shipped in or out

bombardment—an attack with cannons and bombs

campaign—a series of military operations

casualties—persons killed or wounded in a war

capital—the city where the government meets

carpetbagger—the name given to Northerners who went to the South to profit from the defeat of the Confederacy

cavalry—soldiers fighting on horseback

confederacy—a group of states working together

Confederate—referring to the Southern states which left the Union during the Civil War

emancipation—to free slaves

federal—relating to the national government, not the states

flank—the right or left side of a military unit

inauguration—the swearing-in of a president or government official

ironclad—a battleship covered with iron plates

legislature—group of lawmakers who make, change, and repeal laws

musket—a long gun with poorer accuracy than a rifle

orator—public speaker

plantation—a large farm usually with one or two cash crops

proclamation—an official declaration

rebel—someone who fights against the government

Reconstruction—a period of about 10 years after the Civil War

regiment—a unit of soldiers, often about 1,000 troops

scalawags—name given to Southerners who cooperated with Union officials after the war

secede—the decision of a state to leave the Union

siege—to surround an enemy and cut off supplies

skirmish—a short battle with few casualties

slave—a person who is owned by another person

surrender—to give up a fight or war

territory—an area of land which is not yet a state

traitor—someone who helps the enemy

treaty—a formal agreement between nations

Union—the United States of America, during the Civil War this referred to the Northern states

Answer Key

Page 33
1. b
2. d
3. a
4. d
5. c
6. c
7. a
8. b
9. c
10. a

Page 34
1. b
2. c
3. b
4. a
5. b
6. c
7. a
8. b
9. a
10. b

Page 35
1. c
2. c
3. b
4. c
5. b
6. a
7. b
8. d
9. b
10. c

Page 36
1. a
2. c
3. a
4. b
5. b

6. c
7. b
8. c
9. a
10. b

Page 37
1. b
2. d
3. a
4. d
5. b
6. a
7. c
8. d
9. b
10. d

Page 38
1. b
2. c
3. a
4. b
5. c
6. b
7. d
8. b
9. a
10. d

Page 39
1. a
2. d
3. b
4. a
5. c
6. b
7. a
8. c
9. b
10. d

Page 43
1. k
2. j
3. b
4. a
5. c
6. g
7. h
8. e
9. d
10. i
11. f
12. rebels, secede
13. infantry, musket
14. arsenal
15. sentry
16. ironclad, casualties

Page 52
1. Dauphin
2. 21
3. Owen
4. He didn't believe it would succeed.
5. William Lieman and Albert Hazlett
6. Salmon and Jason
7. Mrs. Huffmaster
8. the death of her sister Amelia
9. She was sold back into slavery.
10. He was captured, convicted of treason, and hanged.

Answer Key *(cont.)*

Page 69

Union States

1. California
2. Connecticut
3. Delaware
4. Illinois
5. Indiana
6. Iowa
7. Kansas
8. Kentucky
9. Maine
10. Maryland
11. Massachusetts
12. Michigan
13. Minnesota
14. Missouri
15. New Hampshire
16. New Jersey
17. New York
18. Ohio
19. Oregon
20. Pennsylvania
21. Rhode Island
22. Vermont
23. Wisconsin

Confederate States

1. Alabama
2. Arkansas
3. Florida
4. Georgia
5. Louisiana
6. Mississippi
7. North Carolina
8. South Carolina
9. Tennessee
10. Texas
11. Virginia

Page 70

1. Mobile Bay
2. Atlanta, Chickamauga
3. Antietam
4. Vicksburg
5. Gettysburg
6. Fort Sumter
7. Chattanooga, Fort Donelson, Shiloh
8. Bull Run, Chancellorsville, Cold Harbor, Fredericksburg, Petersburg, Spotsylvania, Wilderness